The Pearl Poet Revisited

Twayne's English Authors Series

George D. Economou, Editor

University of Oklahoma

TEAS 512

THE DREAMER ACROSS THE RIVER FROM THE PEARL MAIDEN, BL MS
COTTON NERO A.X., FOLIO 42.
Photograph by permission of the British Library.

The Pearl Poet Revisited

Sandra Pierson Prior

Columbia University

Twayne Publishers • New York
Maxwell Macmillan Canada • Toronto
Maxwell Macmillan International • New York Oxford Singapore Sydney

Twayne's English Authors Series No. 512

The Pearl Poet Revisited
Sandra Pierson Prior

Copyright © 1994 by Twayne Publishers

Twayne Publishers
Macmillan Publishing Company
866 Third Avenue
New York, New York 10022

Maxwell Macmillan Canada, Inc.
1200 Eglinton Avenue East
Suite 200
Don Mills, Ontario M3C 3N1

Library of Congress Cataloging-in-Publication Data

Prior, Sandra Pierson.
 The pearl poet revisited / Sandra Pierson Prior.
  p.   cm.—(Twayne's English authors series)
 Includes bibliographical references (p.) and index.
  ISBN 0-8057-4516-5
 1. English poetry—Middle English, 1110–1500—History and criticism. 2. Gawain (Legendary character)—Romances—History and criticism. 3. Manuscripts, English (Middle)—England—West Midlands. 4. Patience (Middle English poem) 5. Purity (Middle English poem) 6. Gawain and the Grene Knight. 7. Pearl (Middle English poem) I. Title.
PR1972.G353P75   1992
821'.1—dc20   94-14519
                                                                     CIP

10 9 8 7 6 5 4 3 2 1 (hc)

Printed in the United States of America

Contents

Acknowledgements

I would like to thank the University of Chicago Press for permission to use portions of my article, *"Patience*—Beyond Apocalypse," in chapter 4 of this study. The article originally appeared in *Modern Philology* 83 (1986): 337–48. (Copyright © 1986 by the University of Chicago Press. All rights reserved. Reprinted by permission of the University of Chicago Press.) The British Library has provided the photograph and kindly granted permission to reproduce the illustration of the Dreamer in *Pearl,* which is from the manuscript containing the Pearl poet's works: BL MS Cotton Nero A.x., folio 42.

Chronology

Many of these dates are approximate and those for literary texts are often a matter of scholarly dispute—in the latter case, I have usually given the date that represents recent scholarly consensus.

early 4th c.	Eusebius, *The History of the Church*
354–430	St. Augustine
ca. 520–524	Boethius, *Consolation of Philosophy*
ca. 800	Nennius, *Historia Britonum*
1066	Norman Invasion of England
ca. 1136–38	Geoffrey of Monmouth, *The History of the Kings of Britain*
1160s?	Marie de France, *Lais*
ca. 1169–80	Chrétien de Troyes, *Erec and Enide, Cligés, Yvain, Lancelot*
ca. 1230–35	Guillaume de Lorris, *The Romance of the Rose* (first part, lines 1–4058)
ca. 1275	Jean de Meun, *The Romance of the Rose* (second part, lines 4059–21,780)
ca. 1290	*Guy of Warwick, Beves of Hamtoun, Richard Coeur de Lion* (early Middle English romances about English heroes)
ca. 1307–21	Dante Alighieri, *The Divine Comedy*
1327–77	Reign of Edward III
1328–1384	John Wyclif
1330?–1408	John Gower
1332?–1400?	William Langland
1337	Beginning of Hundred Years' War
1343?–1400	Geoffrey Chaucer
1346–49	Black Death (first of several outbreaks that continued through the following decades)

Chapter One

The Pearl Poet and His Time and Place

The name and identity of the writer we now call the "Pearl poet" or the "Gawain poet" is not known to us. We infer his existence from four poems that are found gathered together in one manuscript held in the British Library. Like many medieval literary works, the four poems in the manuscript bear no titles of their own. Modern editors of the texts have since given them titles, all but the last taken from the most focal word in the first line of its respective poem. In the order they appear in the manuscript, these poems are *Pearl, Cleanness* (sometimes called *Purity*), *Patience,* and *Sir Gawain and the Green Knight.* Two of the poems, *Cleanness* and *Patience,* are retellings of biblical narratives: *Cleanness* of several Old Testament stories, primarily from Genesis, and *Patience* of the story of Jonah. *Pearl,* the first poem in the manuscript, is a dream poem that describes the visionary experiences of a grief-stricken narrator. And, finally, *Gawain,* the most famous of the four, is an Arthurian romance that recounts the adventures of Gawain and his encounter with the Green Knight.

The language of the poems is essentially the dialect of Middle English used in the northwest Midlands around 1400; thus the poet and his original audience were presumably from that region, roughly the northern half of the West Midlands, which is, as its name indicates, the western half (actually it is less than half—the East Midlands occupies a much bigger chunk) of the area of England north of London and south of Northumbria.[1] The manuscript itself, part of the Cotton collection in the British Library and cataloged as MS Cotton Nero A.x., is a scruffy little thing: a small book, with pages measuring about seven by five inches, written in a crabbed, hard-to-read Gothic hand, and illustrated with 12 pictures, all rather crudely done. Perhaps no one cared enough about the poems to have them copied in a more impressive format, but it is more likely the case that at one time there existed richer, more elaborate manuscripts of one or all of these poems, manuscripts that have long since been lost to us.

In fact, we are fortunate that this manuscript survived at all. Given its size and seeming insignificance it might easily have been overlooked and lost, were it not for the efforts of one or two Renaissance antiquarians. Sir Robert Cotton, a preeminent Renaissance book collector (1571–1631), acquired the manuscript containing the Pearl poet's works for his collection, apparently getting it from Henry Saville of Yorkshire (1568–1617), whose library catalog provides the first explicit mention we have of the manuscript. Cotton's impressive collection, which included many of our most important medieval English manuscripts (among them the sole surviving manuscript of *Beowulf,* as well as of other Old English poems), was later given to Britain and eventually stored in Asburnham House. The somewhat unusual name of the manuscript for the Pearl poems, Cotton Nero A.x., is a survival of the original cataloging system for Cotton's library. The presses in which books were shelved were identified by the busts of Roman emperors and other ancient rulers—Cleopatra, Junius, Nero, and others—that rested on top of the cases. Within each press, capital letters and lowercase roman numerals further designated the manuscripts; hence, the Pearl poet's works were bound in the tenth book, of the A division, in the press under the bust of Nero.

In 1731, exactly one hundred years after Cotton's death, there was a terrible fire in Asburnham House, and many of the manuscripts were badly damaged, some even destroyed (Cotton Vitellius A.xv., the manuscript that contained *Beowulf,* was among those scorched—others incurred worse damage). Cotton Nero A.x., however, escaped any effects from the fire. It did suffer subsequently, though, from lack of attention. There is little indication that anyone noticed, much less read, the poems contained in it for another hundred years, until 1839 when Sir Frederic Madden first published *Sir Gawain and the Green Knight,* together with other romances about Gawain. It was still another generation before the three other poems, *Pearl, Cleanness,* and *Patience,* were published by Richard Morris in 1864.

There is no indication in the original manuscript as to who composed these poems, nor do we have any evidence from outside the manuscript, such as references in other poems or in extraliterary documents, that would aid us in identifying the poet. We do not even know for certain if all four poems are the work of one poet; indeed, some scholars believe they are not. The poems could be the product of two poets, or even of a small "school" of poets. It is unlikely that they are the oral compositions of a community: they are far too "literary" and do not have the typical characteristics of oral compositions, which would have been molded and adapted through recitations over the years before they chanced to be written down.

Despite the lack of certain proof, the majority of scholars and critics believe that in this manuscript, Cotton Nero A.x., we have the poems of a single poet, who, while drawing on many sources and traditions, carefully crafted his poems into the unique works of art that have come down to us. Recited to a present audience they certainly were. And they may well have been revised and modified several times, whether by the poet himself, or by other performers/reciters, or by later scribes and compilers.[2] Thus the unique versions of each poem that now exist may not be the last or the best of the several that may have been recited or written. If we had additional versions, we could compare them with each other (as we do with many other medieval texts) in order to determine the poet's own "text," assuming, of course, that the poet had one final text for each poem (which is not necessarily the case). Even when there is only a single surviving version of a medieval author's work, scholars have some fairly reliable ways of determining what changes (intentional or otherwise) a scribe might have made in the poet's "original."[3] These changes, however, are usually a matter of words or phrases, occasionally a whole line or two, rarely more. For example, there is one place in the poems of the *Pearl* manuscript where an entire line seems to have been omitted, another place where the proper order of the lines has apparently been jumbled, and still another place in *Pearl* where some scholars have thought that a complete 12-line stanza had been added—but no one much believes that anymore.[4] Aside from these few instances and a number of apparently omitted, added, or misspelled words, generally what differences there may be between the poems we read and the ones the poet wrote are as unknown as the poet's name.

Ricardian England: The Pearl Poet's Time and Place

Although we lack external information about the poems and their poet, scholars have been able to glean, from both the manuscript and the texts themselves, enough evidence to place the Pearl poet in the latter part of the fourteenth century. This means that the Pearl poet was writing at the same time as Chaucer, Langland, and Gower, a period that has been dubbed "Ricardian" by J. A. Burrow (following the tendency we have to name English literary periods after the monarch reigning at the time, as with "Elizabethan" or "Victorian").[5]

The term "Ricardian" is a bit problematic, however. For one thing, Edward III reigned for 50 years (1327–77), well past midcentury, and his influence on English culture and society was powerful enough that much of late fourteenth-century England is at least as "Edwardian" as it is "Ricardian." Thus, insofar as we can date the major poets of the "Ricardian" period, we would probably have them at least beginning their careers under Edward's reign. Furthermore, even when Richard II did become king, he was underage and therefore not personally ruling the country for the first half of his official reign. However, the last quarter of the fourteenth century did in fact roughly coincide with the reign of Richard II, which lasted from 1377 to 1399. Furthermore, it was this reign that witnessed the flourishing of the major Middle English poets: Chaucer, Langland, Gower, and the Pearl poet. For these reasons, and in the interest of simplicity, "Ricardian" seems as good a label as any for this period. Certainly, some such label seems useful, for it draws attention to the importance of the latter part of the fourteenth century in English history and literature. In addition to its important literary output, the Ricardian period was characterized by some extraordinary political, economic, social, and cultural developments—some that were signs of prosperity and growth, some that were clearly disasters, and many that were both threatening and exciting.

In addition to the power struggles among the ruling classes, which eventually led to the War of the Roses in the next century, England throughout the fourteenth century was engaged in territorial warfare over holdings in the corners of the British Isles and in France and the Low Countries. These recurring battles brought prestige and booty when successful (as in the earlier part of Edward III's reign), but drained the country's energies and finances and angered its people when English armies lost. It is not uncommon to view these battles as dynastic quarrels, which in many ways they were, but they also were not unconnected to the lower classes and the middle classes, both of which not only bore the burden in taxes, but also profited from the opportunity for remuneration through warfare, either directly by fighting or indirectly by supplying the military. Moreover, many of the battles on the Continent concerned areas critical to England's wool trade and therefore were important to the merchant classes.

Apart from the mixed blessings of warfare, the last quarter of the fourteenth century was marked by social unrest, much of it the direct or indirect result of the labor shortage brought about by several plague epidemics that started in midcentury. Although the demand for labor would seem to be a good thing for peasants and workers (primarily agrarian), the resulting increase in bargaining power for laborers prompted by a significant drop in their numbers was offset by the reactionary repressive measures taken by the frightened landed classes. Nonetheless, in the second half of the fourteenth century English society did, in fact, become more mobile, both literally and figuratively. Peasants did not stay for generations in the same geographical place, but—often to the horror of their rulers—moved around in search of better wages and conditions. Along with this physical mobility went a small measure of social and economic mobility (small in comparison to the modern myth of "rags-to-riches" in one or two generations, that is).

This social mobility coincided with the beginnings of a merchant economy and the growth of London, which was emerging as the heart of England's urban, merchant culture. London also was the center of political power—even nobles with major holdings far from London regularly spent time there. The city thus brought together two quite different societies and cultures: the courtly one associated with the royal family, and the middle-class one based on the merchant economy and the professional classes, including lawyers and scribes (this being the time when books began to be produced by commercial scriptoria, rather than by monasteries and other religious institutions).

The backgrounds and interests of the Ricardian poets reflect their exciting, socially volatile times, as well as demonstrate its artistic and literary richness. While we know almost as little about Langland as we do about the Pearl poet, Chaucer and Gower figure in documents and records outside their own poetry. The information on Chaucer, in particular, though scanty by modern standards, is sufficient to indicate in broad outlines that his life, like his poetry, was characterized by a mixture of the London, merchant world with an older, more traditional, more aristocratic, more learned, and more continental one. Although Chaucer worked as a middle-class professional, he obtained his jobs primarily because he was a very successful medieval courtier. (It is particularly remarkable in view of the political struggles and enmity surrounding the English throne and the royal family that Chaucer managed to enjoy the favor of so many different factions and to have received patronage both from Richard and from his cousin Henry IV, by whom Richard was deposed.)

A similar mixture of classes and cultures can be found in Chaucer's poetry, which provides evidence of how firmly and explicitly Ricardian literature could be set in its contemporary culture and still draw on a rich tradition of learning and courtly traditions. Chaucer's most famous poem, *The Canterbury Tales,* contains many figures, particularly among the pilgrims, who belong to what can only be called the medieval middle class—the Wife of Bath, the Merchant, and the Sergeant of Law, for example. On the other hand, this same poem also includes pilgrims, like the Knight and the Squire, who belong more properly to the landed classes (but who are well below royalty); more significantly *The Canterbury Tales* includes stories of and from the courtly culture, stories about kings and knights and their adventures of love. Several of Chaucer's other poems, especially the early ones, are dedicated, or at least directed, to Plantagenet patrons. These, and the magnificent *Troilus and Criseyde,* presume an audience composed of the cultural elite: the learning behind these poems is vast, especially in astrology and rhetoric; they offer stories told either in the latest French and Italian forms or in some of the oldest and best classical ones; and they play with those forms in a highly sophisticated manner.

The courtly culture of Chaucer's poetry also reflects the importance of chivalry to late medieval England. While proponents of an older view, Huizinga, for example, have argued that chivalry was in its decline by the late Middle Ages (having become a matter of ceremony and impractical ideals, while real warfare had turned brutal and ugly),[6] most scholars now believe that the end of the medieval period not only produced a wealth of new chivalric institutions and values, but that the relationship between these and actual warfare was not at all simple. The very questions of what chivalry is (beyond its most reductive definition as the culture of a mounted warrior class) and whether it was declining are not new to modern scholarship, but in fact are contained in the literature of the late Middle Ages itself, both in the treatises on chivalry and also in the period's romances and histories that focus on chivalric values. As Chickering puts it, "[P]erhaps the most characteristic aspect of chivalric literature is its own historical self-consciousness."[7]

The practice of warfare, the values of those who engaged in it, their heroes, and the stories or histories of those heroes greatly absorbed the interest of the ruling class of England (and France) in the fourteenth century. In the mid-fourteenth century (ca. 1348), Edward III founded the Order of the Garter, the oldest and most prestigious chivalric order in England;[8] In his *Chronicles,* Jean Froissart recorded detailed accounts of many chivalric ceremonies and tournaments;[9] and a bit later, at the beginning of the fifteenth century, a woman, Christine de Pizan, wrote *Le Livre des daits d'armes et de chevalerie* (The book of deeds of arms and of chivalry), a treatise on chivalry.[10]

Christine's role as the author of a chivalric treatise is unusual since women were outsiders to the culture of chivalry: they could not be warriors, fight in tournaments, become members of chivalric orders, or even, except at secondhand, be praised for their chivalric virtues. On the other hand, Christine's treatise is primarily a book on decorum and manners and as such shares certain features with the many courtesy books produced at this time—these were manuals of behavior for the upper classes (probably one sure indication that there must have been some new members who were "not to the manner born" and thus needed guidance on the deportment that should have come naturally to the truly noble). Furthermore, Christine's role as the author of a chivalric text fits with our sense that chivalry involves the relationship of men and women at least as much as it concerns codes of conduct in warfare. Certainly, in the fourteenth century a knight's manners and behavior towards women, especially in love affairs, lie at the center of many romances, especially the more courtly ones. Chaucer's Squire, the son of the pilgrim Knight in *The Canterbury Tales,* epitomizes the genteel manners commonly associated with chivalry: he is praised for his grace and skill in singing, dancing, and versifying, and we are told that all his deeds of battle are done so as "to stonden in his lady grace" (to stand in his lady's favor. *The Canterbury Tales*, The General Prologue, line 88).

The pilgrimage framing narrative of *The Canterbury Tales* further suggests that the chivalric, courtly culture and the urban, middle-class one were intertwined with the ecclesiastical culture of fourteenth-century England, a culture that participated in both the unrest and the rich development found in the cities and the courts. In addition to the more arcane theological debates being waged by churchmen and theologians in the Pearl poet's time, several issues were a matter of concern to laypeople as well as to ecclesiastics, and many of them were at the center of heretical movements. These larger issues—translating the Bible into English, the role and practice of the sacraments, where and how the church got its wealth and what the church did with it, who received ecclesiastical appointments and how, and the role and place of the orders of friars—all involved the laity directly and affected their religious practices and their relationship to the church. Thus it is not surprising that these matters became social and political issues as well as theological ones, and that the more worldly aspects of religious controversy are given an ironic and satiric perspective in *The Canterbury Tales.*

While Chaucer's life and poetry provide us with the broadest and most comprehensive picture of the culture of late medieval England, other major poets, especially Langland and Gower, provide us with details, often fuller ones, about particular aspects of their culture. The same intellectual and highly cultural ambience that characterizes much of Chaucer's poetry is suggested by Gower's poetry too, which, while it lacks Chaucer's subtle artistry, nonetheless presumes an audience familiar with courtly literary forms and classical traditions. Gower's *Confessio Amantis* incorporates both his own era's most sophisticated literary forms and conventions—it is a dream vision allegory—and classical tales and traditions. Langland's poem, *Piers Plowman,* on the other hand, while it contains an immense fund of learning, is chiefly characterized by an anti-intellectual and anti-aristocratic fervor. The satire of *Piers* gains much of its force from its demonstrated familiarity with a wide range of four-teenth-century forms of English culture—everything from the corrupt workings of the royal court, to the failure of the agrarian society to pro-duce food, to the pompous posturings of ecclesiastical preachers.

We see, then, that much of the culture of late medieval England is reflected in its poetry. But poetry is itself a part of culture, not just a mir-ror standing outside of culture. In fact, because the Ricardian period was characterized by dramatic changes in language, prosody, and book pro-duction, it could be argued that literature was at the center of the major cultural development in late fourteenth-century England. Moreover, in seeking to place an unidentified poet, like the Pearl poet, within his cul-ture, the only reasonably accurate information we can work with is his literary and linguistic context, since they can be directly connected to his poems.

The Pearl Poet's Linguistic and Literary Environment

What, then, was the linguistic situation in the Pearl poet's time? Early in the fourteenth century there were many spoken dialects of English, but written English was still not in much use, and had not been since the Norman Conquest in 1066. Latin continued to be the preferred language for learning and biblical and theological study, while French, especially in its Anglo-Norman dialect, remained the language of most aristocratic pursuits, like hunting and heraldry. In the latter part of the fourteenth century English began to make a gradual comeback, first as a spoken language for the English ruling classes and by the end of the cen-tury even as a written language, one increasingly used in the courts and in civic records.[11] The Norman nobles had probably needed to use some bits of English all along in order to do business with the peasant and working classes who knew no French and Latin, but the ruling class's knowledge and use of English increased greatly in the Pearl poet's time. One oft-cited example of this change is the fact that in 1362 Edward III addressed Parliament in English, another that in this same year Parliament ruled that henceforth all legal proceedings were to be conducted in English (because so few parties could understand French) (Fisher 1992, 1169). By Henry IV's reign (which began in 1399), most of the business of governing was being done in English.[12]

In addition to emerging as the language of court, governance, and business, English began to replace Anglo-Norman as the language of courtly literature. However, the English that emerges in even the most courtly literature (Chaucer's, for example) is an English profoundly changed from that used by the Anglo-Saxons in 1066. English is in its roots a Germanic language and originally, like other Germanic languages, was highly inflected (that is, it changed the forms of verbs, nouns, pronouns, and modifiers to indicate grammatical function). But by the late Middle Ages English had all but ceased to decline its nouns and substantives and had been forced therefore to rely more on word order to establish syntax. This loss of inflections was caused partly by linguistic factors in Anglo-Saxon itself, but it was certainly hastened by its long exposure to French from the time of the Norman Conquest to the late fourteenth century.[13]

Along with these changes in its grammar and syntax, English absorbed and was in fact still absorbing much of the vocabulary of both French and Latin (the latter primarily via French). This whole process was not completed by the Pearl poet's time, when the various English dialects were extremely unstable in their forms and spellings. The result for us is a language that is often very difficult, especially in dialects such as that used by the Pearl poet that are far removed from the London-area dialect, which is the ancestor of modern English. Even in the Ricardian period this instability and variety of language must have been confusing and a hindrance to clear communication, but it also provided unique opportunities for poets to capitalize on the multiple forms and meanings of words, giving them a rich storehouse that could be adapted to the demands of the verse and general literary contexts. Borrowing "frenchified" words, for example, often was necessary when English had no word for something—which was especially true when a poet wrote on chivalric or courtly topics; other times a French-based word may have served simply to signal a courtly milieu.

Apart from the language itself, the literature shows a similar mixture of English and French traditions. While the Anglo-Norman and French literary traditions were clearly important to late Ricardian poets, the Pearl poet and his contemporaries also drew upon the native English literary tradition, which, since the eleventh century, had stayed in the background. This tradition, which in the late Middle Ages existed more in oral and popular forms than in written ones, was inherited from the great flowering of Anglo-Saxon language and poetry, at base also an oral culture but one that had been carefully written down and preserved by Anglo-Saxon scribes, mostly just prior to the Norman Conquest (and some even afterward). The native tradition that survived into the fourteenth century consisted principally of the Anglo-Saxon alliterative verse form,[14] and a preference for dramatic and action-filled narrative poems about biblical and legendary heroes and heroines. There are some Old English poems of a different kind, for example, elegies like *The Wanderer,* that are meditative and quietly sorrowful, but this genre seems not to have lasted (or to have been appreciated) in Middle English culture. Most Middle English narrative poetry, especially of the popular kind, lacks the grandeur and heroic sweep of Old English poems like *Beowulf* and *Judith,* but romances like *King Horn* and *Havelok* do tell good stories, with plenty of action.[15]

In addition to the Anglo-Saxon poetic tradition, the Celtic languages and cultures of the British isles provided an important native strain of a different kind. This strain mostly makes its way into medieval English literature in the form of bits of tales and myths or names of characters, especially those associated with King Arthur. The Celtic influence is difficult to trace, since whatever ancient Celtic traditions were transmitted to late medieval England did so primarily orally, or in written texts that have not survived, so we have few manuscripts that antedate the Middle English texts that might have been based on Celtic sources. Those that do are preserved in the Welsh and Irish languages and seem either to have been little known by Middle English poets or to have been as much the recipient of influence from Middle English and French poems and stories as to have been the source of influence.

The Breton lay is probably the most explicitly Celtic literary form and tradition in Middle English. Apparently originally a short narrative poem sung or recited by the Breton harpers, the Breton lay is earliest and best attested to by Marie de France, who wrote *lais* in French in the late twelfth century. In the Prologue to her *Lais,* Marie says that she decided to set the lais she had heard from the Breton harpers into *dités* (words, a saying, or a song) and into *rimé* (verse).[16] And later, at the close of the lai *Guigemar,* we are told:

> De cest cunte k'oï avez
> Fu *Guigemar* li lais trovez,
> Que hum fait en harpe e en rote;
> Bone en est a oïr la note.
> (Rychner, ed., lines 883–86)

> From this story that you have heard
> the *lai* of Guigemar was composed,
> which is now recited to the harp and rote;
> the music is a pleasure to hear.
> (Ferrante and Hanning trans.)

Over a century later we find similar claims in Middle English texts. For example, in the opening lines of *Kyng Orfew,* the narrator says: "The Brytans, as the boke seys, / Off diverse thingys thei made ther leys" (The Britons, as the book says, made their lays of many different things; 7–8).[17] While the reference to "the boke" in *Kyng Orfew* seems to contradict the usual view that this Celtic tradition was an oral one (Rumble, "Introduction," xii–xv), the narrator here may just be using "book" to suggest authority (as other medieval poets and even historians were apt to do). Or, perhaps by this time the Breton lay had indeed become a "book"—it certainly had been written down, in French and English, though not as far as we know in Breton. In other words, Marie's lais in French, or the several Middle English translations and paraphrases of them, may have been the only lays the poet of *Kyng Orfew* knew. In this Middle English text, even the memory of the oral source may have been lost, or rather it had been transformed into a different kind of authority: a "book."

The Breton lay is illustrative of the rest of Celtic tradition as a source for vernacular literature. What we have today as evidence is not so much the sources and traditions themselves as the assertions of the non-Celtic poets that such traditions existed. It is largely owing to the claims of poets such as Marie de France and Chrétien de Troyes that modern scholars first embarked on their search for Celtic sources. But if we put aside that search and focus rather on its impulse, we come to realize something important about certain medieval texts, especially romances: these stories and their authors and audiences presume the Celtic origins of many of the folk traditions and customs they refer to; therefore, some fairly strong reasons must exist for these claims (one of the reasons, of course, could be that they were true). What was this tradition for these poets? At base it was oral and nonliterate (outside, in particular, the Latin literary culture); it was conveyed in a different language,[18] and finally, it was associated with a different culture with a different set of values and beliefs. Celtic or Welsh or Breton usually suggests pagan in medieval tradition, although it is a paganism quite different from either the Roman or Germanic variety. Even when mixed with (or whitewashed by) Christianity, the Celtic stories and figures retain their pagan trappings; skills and arts become magic (whether white or black), while gods and demons turn into fairies and dwarves and magical creatures like the Hawk-Knight (who is the lover of the heroine in Marie's *Yonec*). In particular, the Celtic strain in Middle English culture tends to be uncourtly, unlearned, and uncivilized. It belongs outside, in the fields and forests, especially in the wilderness—where *wodwos* (trolls) live under rocks, where giants are apt to come crashing down out of the mountains, and where fairies can sometimes be seen dancing in the meadow.

Celtic influence in late medieval England, then, is at once both popular and literary. Its importance is attested to in some of the most literate, up-to-date, and sophisticated poets, but its nature, according to these same poets, is ancient, oral, and folk. A similar mixture of culture and anticulture, or literate and illiterate, exists in the great wealth of religious writings, both prose and verse, from fourteenth- and fifteenth-century English. The Pearl poet's age, the age of some of the greatest English mystics (several, like Juliana of Norwich and the anonymous author of *The Cloud of Unknowing,* writing in English), is one of popular religious fervor, attested to by a number of religious texts, many of which are explicitly aimed at relatively uneducated audiences (often barely literate, or at least not literate in Latin). Mystical and devotional writing by its nature tends to be antitextual or at least supratextual, and antilearning, for its focus is on the individual's personal relationship with God, not on theology or scriptural study. Writers of such texts, whether journals of mystical experiences or moral allegories or devotional lyrics, often insist on their lack of learning, even their illiteracy. (It is not always clear how "true" this illiteracy is, or whether it refers simply to an inability to read and write in Latin.)[19]

Paradoxically, to some extent the impetus and authority for this popular strain aimed at a lay audience comes from learned and scholarly clerics. The Wycliffite movement is a typical example of this mixture. John Wycliff himself was a learned Oxford cleric, who engaged in some fairly arcane scholarly debates, most of which got him into trouble with the church hierarchy. The Wycliffite Bible, whatever part Wycliff himself may have played in its translation (he probably translated the Gospels) (Partridge 335), could only have been produced by those capable of reading and translating Latin. On the other hand, the project itself was part of Wycliff's general view that the common folk mattered and had a right to read the Scriptures in their native tongue, a view that quite easily merged with populist and anti-intellectual attitudes.

In addition to the translation of the Bible, there were Middle English paraphrases or retellings of biblical stories that appeared separately or within larger texts; again, though aimed perhaps at an audience unable to read the Bible in Latin, these retellings usually demonstrate their authors' learned familiarity with the biblical texts. Such renderings on a grand scale can be found in the English cycle drama, which we know to be beginning in the late fourteenth century even though our earliest surviving texts do not go back that far.[20] Cycle drama is the product of an even more complicated mixture of clerical and popular cultures than other popularized religious texts. Performed by a mixed group of civic organizations and aimed at a large and often minimally educated audience, the mystery plays were, however, conceived and written by those who were themselves not just literate, but well-read in both the Bible and its medieval interpretations and also clearly well aware of the current controversies in Christian teaching. Similarly, among some of our finest religious lyrics are many that were written by clerics, even though these lyrics quite clearly were intended for the laity.[21]

Much of this religious writing in Middle English dialects and popular forms can be viewed as an impulse, often quite conscious, not just to popularize, but also to anglicize, literature and learning, to free both from the inaccessibility of Latin and continental languages. This impulse is not confined to composing in English, or to translating and compiling from Latin and continental languages into English. The interest in making much literary culture more English, not just more available to the less learned, is demonstrated by less obvious, but significant trends: the adaptation of a continental literary genre like dream vision or romance to an English variation; the revival of native (that is, Old English) literary forms, most particularly that of alliterative verse, little in evidence since the Norman Conquest; the reclaiming as English (or "British") of Arthurian and Celtic tales and figures; and the development of some new and very English literary forms—Chaucer's two favorite verse forms, iambic pentameter couplets and rime royale (a seven-line stanza, rhyming *ababbcc*) and the cycle drama, for example.

The Pearl Poet

This, then, was the cultural, especially the literary, context in which the Pearl poet was writing: a newly emerging English literature and language, which while drawing on three older traditions—Anglo-Saxon, Celtic, and continental (especially French and Latin via French)—also was influenced by its contemporary political and social surroundings. These surroundings include the beginnings of an urban culture, the movement toward a more anglicized ruling class and political identity, and the radical changes in the English language, primarily wrought by its prolonged exposure to dialects of French. Where does the Pearl poet fit into this setting? Or more precisely, since he himself cannot be identified, much less be given a definite historical place, what can we infer about him from his poems and where do his poems fit into late-four-teenth-century English culture?

Not only does the dialect of the poems place the poet and his audience in the northwest region of the Midlands, it also tells us something about their social class.[22] The fact that the language of his poems is not exactly the same as any spoken dialect, but is instead a poetic language containing many borrowings from more northern dialects and even from Old Norse, as well as from dialects of French, especially Anglo-Norman, suggests that we are dealing with a cultured and well-read poet who expected a similar audience. In addition, the language of the Cotton Nero manuscript, like its general appearance, has a somewhat old-fashioned and provincial air, suggesting a certain distance from London and from much that in Chaucer's time constituted the cosmopolitan and the urban.

On the other hand, we should not confuse "provincial" with "rural backwater," or "noncosmopolitan" with "ignorant" or "unlettered," or "nonurban" with "peasant." In fact, the Pearl poet's works are filled with bits of learning (especially biblical and religious learning), while *Sir Gawain and the Green Knight* in particular is a very courtly poem, with aristocratic lords and ladies doing aristocratic things like hunting and feasting. Moreover, these are not poems written in popular forms, but works that are tightly crafted and very literary in their form and genre, works that require careful attention, even from an audience more at ease with their language, especially from a listening audience.

We must assume, then, a courtly audience with leisure to enjoy these poems—perhaps a court at some distance from London, in the fourteenth-century equivalent of a country retreat, but still versed in the latest styles and manners. The Pearl poet's original audience may well have been an actual court, an aristocratic one that included nobles who, like John of Gaunt, had been in London and elsewhere, even perhaps on the Continent—in fact, Gaunt himself might well have been the Pearl poet's patron, or at least a member of his earliest audience, since the poet's dialect places him close to Lancaster.[23]

While the poet's original audience must have been people of elegant taste, familiar with the highly regulated and stylized Norman pursuits of heraldry and hunting, they apparently could also concern themselves with serious moral and religious issues. The literature they read and listened to would have included lyric poems, religious and moral treatises, saints' lives, ballads, various kinds of allegory—especially in the popular medieval genre of the dream poem—and finally romances, both popular ballad-like English ones, many no doubt in the tail-rhyme stanza form mocked by Chaucer in his Tale of Sir Thopas in *The Canterbury Tales,* and more aristocratic ones, including those written in French and Anglo-Norman.

This literary context fits the Pearl poet's works better than the social and political one of fourteenth-century England. For none of the poems in the manuscript is set in the world and time around the poet. *Patience* and *Cleanness* belong to the prechristian, biblical past, *Gawain* to the legendary and romantic time of Arthur and the Round Table. Even *Pearl,* which fictionally at least begins and ends in the poet's lifetime, largely unfolds in his dream, and dreamtime is as distant from "present" England as is Arthur's kingdom. Furthermore, unlike many English dream visions—Chaucer's *Parliament of Fowls,* the anonymous *Winner and Waster,* and Langland's *Piers Plowman,* for example—*Pearl* does not let the public, outside world into the Dreamer's dream, which in the Pearl poet's case is wholly concerned with the Dreamer's own private crisis and its relationship to the Christian truths that are recorded in the Bible.

However, while the Pearl poet seems to stand aside from most of the social and political issues of his time and place, in certain aspects of his poetry he is quite up-to-date. Using the alliterative verse that was proving once again such a viable and popular form for English verse, the Pearl poet also employs syllabic verse and complex rhyme schemes, with a skill and virtuosity virtually unmatched by his peers writing in English. (Chaucer, supremely skillful versifier that he is, did not attempt to combine syllabic rhymed verse with native alliterative forms, with the single exception of a brief passage in his Knight's Tale [I.2603–16].[24]) Another feature of the Pearl poet's craft—detailed descriptions that Burrow calls "pointing" (Burrow 1971, 69–75)—is characteristic of the latest and best of fourteenth-century poetry, although none equals the Pearl poet in his mastery of visual description.[25]

The Pearl poet also is markedly "modern" in his combination of seemingly disparate traditions of literate learning and orality (the latter quite clearly mostly a fiction for him). The Middle English romance, for example, could be either a popular, minstrel form or a sophisticated continental one, depending upon the audience and mileu (Burrow 1982, 50–52). The Pearl poet's romance, *Sir Gawain and the Green Knight,* apparently intended for a sophisticated audience, acknowledges the courtly romance tradition going back to the twelfth century (mostly by self-consciously playing with that tradition), while also creating the illusion of a minstrel retelling a good story he heard around court to an audience of listeners. The two biblical poems, *Patience* and *Cleanness,* reflect a different combination of learned and popular traditions. As we have seen, the act of retelling biblical stories in the vernacular was both a part of the popularizing effort and a task demanding a literate storyteller well-versed in the Bible and in biblical study—certainly the case when the retellings are as detailed as those of the Pearl poet's.

The Pearl poet's brilliant craft in versification and language is another sign of his sophistication and his awareness of the latest literary trends. Except for Langland, who might best be characterized as a poet of artful artlessness, the major Ricardian poets stand apart from their immediate Middle English predecessors in their great attention to craft. Many of the features of the Pearl poet's versification and language are necessarily lost or obscured in translation into modern English, but enough survive, especially in good verse translations, that even those people unable to read the poems in the original can profit from a general knowledge of the verse forms and the poet's techniques of language play. Similarly, the poet's manipulation of syntax and vocabulary, even some of his punning, is apparent, at least in its broadest outlines, in some modern translations. Borroff, in particular, who has translated *Pearl* and *Sir Gawain and the Green Knight,* has done a fine job of imitating the Pearl poet's versification in modern English, although much of the language play is lost in her translations. However, even better than verse translations are texts of the original that are heavily glossed; these should not be too difficult for readers who have some knowledge of Middle English, if only in Chaucer's much easier dialect.

Because I believe so strongly in the centrality of language and versification to the Pearl poet's art, I would like to conclude this chapter with a brief, introductory discussion of these aspects of Middle English poetry. Here, and throughout this book, I will quote in the original, but provide translations (my own, unless otherwise indicated). Even if the nonspecialist prefers to read the Pearl poet's works in translation, this introduction and the quotations in the original should acquaint the reader with the poet's complex craft. My hope is that new readers will be encouraged to try reading at least some of this poetry in the original and perhaps come to see the language as slightly less daunting than it first appears, or at least to find the effort well worth the struggle.[26]

The Pearl Poet's Versification

The metrical unit of the Pearl poet's verse is the alliterative line. This meter, inherited from the Anglo-Saxon *scops* (the Old English word for "poets"), was used by some English poets of the thirteenth and fourteenth centuries, especially those writing in the dialects of the west and north of England. We have no treatise on poetics or rhetoric from the poets practicing this verse form either in Anglo-Saxon times or when the Pearl poet was writing. We must therefore induce the principles of their verse from the surviving poems themselves, although not surprisingly, scholars disagree about these inferred prosody rules.

The English tradition of alliterative verse differs from the more familiar kind of rhyming, syllabic verse in two respects: its meter depends more upon the number of stresses in a line than upon the number of syllables; and it does not employ rhyme (the practice of repeating the sounds at the ends of words) but instead, as its name suggests, alliteration (the repetition of the sounds at the beginning of words). In the poetry of the Anglo-Saxon scop, the alliterative line consists basically of two half-lines separated by a strong caesura (or pause, usually both metrical and syntactical). Each half-line contains two stressed syllables and a varying number of unstressed syllables. Alliteration joins the stressed syllables from one half-line to the next: the first stress of the second half-line alliterates with one or both of the stresses in the first half-line; but all four stresses almost never alliterate—as a rule, the last stress of the line does not alliterate. Within a half-line, the patterns of the stressed and unstressed syllables can vary, but the variations usually conform to a limited number of models. Finally, the units of verse remain the line and the half-line, for, unlike traditions that can use rhyme patterns or lines of varying length to create stanzas, Anglo-Saxon poets, especially in narrative, tend not to group lines into larger patterns (although the written texts may contain signs, such as large capitals, that indicate sections of the narrative).

The Anglo-Saxon poets seem to have been fairly strict about their verse, perhaps about such matters as the acceptable patterns of stressed and unstressed syllables, and more certainly about the rules of what could be stressed and what could alliterate. Although these details are not agreed upon by scholars, there is sufficient regularity in Old English verse that it seems likely that there were rules at the time that were understood by the makers and audiences of poetry. That does not mean that a poet could not break the rules on occasion (intentionally or not), and certainly a scribe could, especially unwittingly—maybe just because of a copying error, but also perhaps because the scribe's dialect differed from the poet's. (We need to keep in mind that we are working with an imperfect record of what was essentially an oral poetry.)

The alliterative verse that had evolved by the Pearl poet's time is less strict than that practiced by the Old English scop—perhaps because the tradition of the meter was less known, but also because the entire language was in such a state of flux that rules were hard to follow, and harder to preserve from the changes of reciters and scribes. For example, unlike Anglo-Saxon verse, Middle English alliterative verse sometimes uses rhyme (as it does in two of the Pearl poet's works: *Pearl* and *Gawain*), and it is occasionally formed into stanzas, either through its rhyme patterns (as in *Pearl*) or through the use of shorter lines to mark the conclusion of a stanza (as in *Gawain*). In addition, the alliterative line of Middle English verse tends to be freer in its meter than that of Old English: in Middle English it is not uncommon for all four stresses to alliterate; sometimes an unstressed syllable also alliterates; and there are quite a few "hypermetric" lines (that is, lines with more than four stresses).

Aside from these changes, most of the overall effects and characteristics of Old English alliterative verse still exist in the Middle English alliterative line, especially in the hands of a master of technique like the Pearl poet. The line itself has a steady, almost incantatory, rhythm (it is thought that the Anglo-Saxon scops accompanied their verse with a harp, perhaps using it primarily as a percussion instrument, to emphasize the beat). This rhythm, produced by the four beats, separated by a strong caesura (the pause between the two half-lines), but united by the alliteration across the caesura, thus gives the rhythm of *two beats, rest, two beats, double rest, two beats,* and so on. The percussive effect could be strengthened, especially for scenes of noisy action like battles or storms or hunts, by keeping the pattern regular, using "hard" alliterating sounds (like *p* or *k*), and perhaps by adding extra alliteration on unstressed syllables or even a fifth stressed syllable. Similarly, the percussive effect could be softened for scenes of meditation or quiet conversation, either by using softer sounds to alliterate (like liquid consonants or vowels) and by decreasing the number of stresses that alliterate, sometimes dispensing with alliteration altogether.

In both Old English and Middle English verse poets required both a ready supply of synonyms to satisfy the demands of alliteration and also some stock phrases (called "formulas")[27] to fill out half-lines with the proper stress and alliterating patterns. (We should remember that when composing most rhymed verse, especially in the prevailing English forms, a poet does not need to pair too many sounds—rhymed couplets, for example, require only two rhyming sounds for every two lines of verse; but in alliterative verse there must be two to four similar sounds in each line.) Obviously, alliterative verse demands a number of synonyms for words used often, such as *knight* or *sword* or *go*; if not, the *sword* can only *swing,* the *knight* can only *knock* (in Middle English *kn* is a single sound made up of *k* and *n*), and only the *gome* (man) can *go*.

The presence of stock phrases and recurring synonyms in alliterative verse creates a poetic diction consisting of phrases and words probably not used much, if at all, in everyday speech. This diction, when combined with the regular strong beat of the alliterative line, lends a formal tone to the poetry and thereby signals a special, elevated, literary world. The effect is similar to the use of the King James Bible in religious rites and services: when we hear this language, we know that we are in a world removed from the modern, the everyday, and the ordinary. There are thus clear advantages to such a poetic style and language; the disadvantages are equally obvious. Especially in the hands of the mediocre, poetic language can sound trite, or pompous, or even meaningless: *lords* are always *in land*; *frekes* (men/warriors) always *ferde on folde* (go on earth). We tend to pass over terms like *doughty swains* (a term parodied by Chaucer as early as the 1380s but still appearing today in pseudomedieval literature)[28] as at best just referring to "men" or at worst plain silly. (How many readers of Harlequin romances or players of "Dungeons and Dragons" have the least idea of what it is to be "doughty" and what the nuances of the word *swain* might be?) In addition to the problems of stock phrases, the steady rhythm of the alliterative line, going on for a couple thousand lines, can be as annoying as a dripping water tap or as infuriating as the pounding disco music of a nextdoor neighbor's stereo.

The Pearl poet escapes these pitfalls of alliterative verse for two reasons: first, he is a supreme master and does not resort more than absolutely necessary to formulas and stock synonyms; and second, he varies the versification both within the line and without, adjusting to the mood and subject of the poem. For example, sometimes the Pearl poet uses stock phrases in predictable places; more often he either uses a stock phrase in an unusual way or uses an unusual phrase where a stock phrase is expected. In addition, when the context demands, the Pearl poet decreases the alliteration in a single line and otherwise deemphasizes the stresses and the caesura; he does this by using softer sounds to alliterate or by bridging the caesura syntactically so that the sense of the line does not allow for much of a pause. These latter variations occur most often in scenes of quiet conversation or solitary thought: for example, in the bedroom scenes between Gawain and Bertilak's Lady, or in much of *Pearl,* which is such a personal and thoughtful poem. On the other hand, in action scenes, like the hunting and feasting in *Gawain* or the destruction of Sodom and Gomorrah in *Cleanness,* the Pearl poet exploits the rousing rhythm of alliterative verse to its fullest extent, equal to the best of any battle scenes in Old English poetry.

Finally, when he so chooses, the Pearl poet also employs rhyme and rhyming patterns—a little in *Gawain,* a lot in *Pearl*—and stanzaic forms—a loose one in *Gawain,* a complex and tightly constructed one in *Pearl*—to group his verse into larger units than the line and half-line. The poet then uses these stanzaic patterns to mark the various stages in the plot and development of the respective poem. The result is verse that is not just a masterful Middle-English blend of Anglo-Norman and Anglo-Saxon poetic traditions, but also poetry that is extraordinarily pleasurable to hear, a quality which is important because that is the way much of the Pearl poet's audience must have "read" his poems: by hearing them read aloud in court or manor hall. And this is the way more of us should read his poetry: out loud whenever possible, or with a mind's ear that is trained to hear poetry read silently. If we do this, we will know and appreciate this (and all) poetry far better and much more deeply.

Chapter Two
Pearl

Pearl, the first poem in the manuscript, is the most personal, and at the same time the most conventional, of the Pearl poet's four works. It belongs to the popular medieval genre of dream vision, a genre that took many forms and was adapted for various purposes: political and social satire, religious and philosophical allegory and instruction, and the description and analysis of romantic love. The narrator of *Pearl* recounts, in the first person, an experience he has while lamenting the loss of his pearl. He falls asleep in a garden and dreams a dream in which he meets a young woman, the Pearl Maiden, apparently his pearl but in a transformed state. The Dreamer and the Pearl Maiden talk (mostly they debate), and then she shows him the New Jerusalem; in the midst of this final vision, the Dreamer wakes up.

In narrating and describing this experience, *Pearl* draws heavily on literary traditions and conventions. It also employs sophisticated verse techniques virtually unparalleled in Middle English literature and creates an ingenious blend of the native English tradition of alliterative verse and the continental practices of rhyming lines and complex stanzaic patterns. To appreciate this poem and to follow the experience it describes, we therefore need to understand something about its literary background and to pay close attention to its versification and language. I will begin with some discussion of *Pearl's* genre and then proceed to examine its poetic craft, that is, its versification and its language techniques.

Pearl and the Genre of Dream Vision

Critics and scholars argue over virtually everything about *Pearl,* including its genre, some claiming that it is a consolation, others that it is primarily didactic, and still others that it belongs to the genre of debate; and earlier in this century many scholars argued over whether the poem ought to be classified as an allegory or as an elegy (although it would certainly seem possible to be both at once).[1] Although the debate over *Pearl's* genre can easily get silly and irrelevant, I do think paying some attention to this issue is helpful, especially to the extent that *Pearl's* genre works with assumptions and conventions unfamiliar to the modern reader. Unquestionably, *Pearl* is a dream vision, for that genre could include virtually all the others mentioned above. The exact kind of dream vision is not so important, since that is a matter less of the genre to which the poem belongs than of its own variation on the genre, a topic to which we will return later in this chapter.

What is the medieval dream vision, from what does it come, and what are its main characteristics? One of the literary sources for the medieval dream vision is the revelatory, or apocalyptic, vision of religious writing, especially John's Apocalypse.[2] Another source is the tradition of the journey to the underworld or otherworld, which is similar to the religious revelatory vision, but has its roots in pagan literature, rather than in the Bible. In medieval literature the two main sources for such revelatory journeys are classical and Celtic, which can be combined, as they are in the Middle English *Sir Orfeo,* a celticized version of the tale of Orpheus's descent to the underworld. Especially popular to medieval readers was *The Dream of Scipio,* which was originally recounted in Cicero's *Republic* but was known to the Middle Ages in an early fifth-century treatise on dream theory written by Macrobius.[3]

A medieval dream vision is almost invariably told in the first person and purports to record an actual dream of the narrator/poet. The poem usually includes, either explicitly or implicitly, some narrative frame that describes the narrator falling asleep in the beginning and then waking up after his dream. Within the dream, the Dreamer wanders in another world, often an ideal landscape, a kind of paradise.[4] In that dream world the Dreamer encounters various figures, some of them allegorical, and at least one authoritative figure who serves as a guide for the Dreamer, either literally by guiding him through the landscape of the dream world, showing him revealing and often predictive scenes, or figuratively by leading him through a discussion of some problem or concern.

While for some time it was fashionable to distinguish between the narrator who tells the dream and the poet who writes the poem, I do not find this distinction to be especially useful, particularly in the case of an anonymous poet like the Pearl poet. A more important distinction is that between the poet/narrator who relates the dream and crafts the poem and the dreamer who dreams the dream. This latter distinction usually (as in the case of Amant [the Lover] in *The Romance of the Rose*) reflects a difference of time and perspective: the narrator looks back upon the dream and sometimes upon events before and after the dream. Such a distinction is, of course, true of most first-person narratives (unless they are the kind that relates events as they happen, like a diary or an epistolary novel), but the distance is greater in dream vision, since the narrator is separated from his dreaming self not just by time, but by mode—the dreamer is in a dream world all his own, while the narrator is in a waking world, the "real" world inhabited by other human beings. The dream vision genre is thus ideal for an examination of the narrator's feelings and inner thoughts and usually begins with some kind of emotional or intellectual crisis. (The similarity to Freudian and Jungian analysis is obvious, and one scholar, Paul Piehler, has written an intriguing study of the genre that draws on Jungian principles.[5])

For some of the more self-conscious poets, the genre of dream vision provided an opportunity to examine their poetic craft and their role as poets. Chaucer, for example, as Robert Payne has demonstrated, used his several dream visions, especially the Prologue to *The Legend of Good Women,* as opportunities to consider the literary sources and techniques of his poetry.[6] Other dream visions concern a religious or philosophical truth; while they often begin with a personal problem, they soon move to broader issues, such as the nature of the good (as in Boethius's *Consolation of Philosophy*) or of salvation (as in Langland's *Piers Plowman*). In addition, dream poems, especially those of the late Middle Ages, could focus exclusively on romantic love (and are thus sometimes labeled "love visions"). The thirteenth-century *Romance of the Rose* is the prime example, in fact the model and archetype, of the love vision. This kind of dream poem, which is much like the more religious and philosophical visions, usually includes a dream world consisting of a paradisiacal garden, allegorical figures and objects that inhabit the dream world, authoritive guides who teach the dreamer, and dialogues or debates between the figures within the dream or the dreamer and a guide. However, instead of considering a question like the nature of salvation, a love vision's ostensible subject is romantic and sexual love (usually, but not always, the dreamer's own love concerns). In *The Romance of the Rose,* the first part (approximately 4,000 lines), which was written by Guillaume de Lorris, focuses on the dreamer's experience of desire—falling in love with the Rose and unsuccessfully trying to get closer to it/her. The poem breaks off while the poet is lamenting the imprisonment of Fair Welcoming, one of his advocates on behalf of the Rose. In the much longer part (more than 17,000 additional lines), written a generation later by Jean de Meun, the dreamer's experience in the garden becomes a vehicle for an encyclopedic discussion not just of all aspects of love, but of a range of other topics. The Lover speaks with several different guides, who often tell stories to illustrate their lessons.

The Romance of the Rose was an immensely popular work. It was widely read, frequently copied and illustrated, translated, paraphrased, imitated, and borrowed from or argued with, perhaps most famously over 100 years later, by Christine de Pisan, who rebutted the antifeminism of Jean de Meun's poem and sources. In the fourteenth-century the Pearl poet's English contemporaries, Chaucer and Gower, as well as several French poets (Guillaume de Machaut and Jean Froissart, for example) wrote love visions, all of them influenced to some extent by *The Romance of the Rose*.

Since many dream poems concern a problem (usually of a religious, philosophical, or romantic nature) that is addressed within the dream, they are often like classical consolations, for example, Boethius's *Consolation of Philosophy*. If the problem is the death of a beloved, the dream poem tends to be elegaic, as well as consolatory; that is, the poem usually combines a celebratory memorial of the beloved with an expression of the dreamer's grief. The consolatory dream vision is one example of how the common medieval habit of conflating Judeo-Christian traditions with those of classical antiquity can be awkward and difficult. Classical texts tend to use journeys to the underworld and dialogues with the dead in a different way, at once both more realistic and more mythical, than do Christian texts. Classical otherworlds are geographical places, reached usually by taking a long journey across land or sea, or more often by descending into the earth; even when, as in *The Dream of Scipio,* one ascends to the afterlife, it tends to be a more physical place than the Christian heaven. On the other hand, in the Christian worldview, heaven is more "real" than this earth and the people there are living (indeed, are more alive than we mortals). The Christian can never view the afterlife as a simple metaphor or literary device, nor can he expect to go to the otherworld without some extraordinary divine dispensation (as Dante is told has been granted to him); getting there involves at least as much change in consciousness as movement through space. Moreover, speaking to the dead means knowing whether they have been saved or not, and if they have been saved, of depicting the life of the blessed. For orthodox Christian poets the danger of being presumptuous when writing about the afterlife and the dead is always present. Even mystics are usually troubled and doubtful about the truth and validity of their visions.

In most respects *Pearl* is very typical of the rather amorphous genre of dream vision. In fact, much of the critical and scholarly debate about this poem arises because *Pearl* draws on so many of these traditions: the religious, revelatory vision; the philosophical/theological dialogue within a dream; and the love vision. On the one hand, *Pearl* contains an authority figure, who guides the Dreamer, first through a theological debate and later to a revelatory vision. On the other hand, much of the poem's language and conventions, in the beginning especially, are characteristic of love visions—the beautiful landscape, the *luf-longyng* (desire) felt by the Dreamer, the conventional terms used for his pearl.[7] *Pearl* is certainly elegaic, because it concerns the death of a loved one, but it is also a consolation, at least in the way it considers the problem of the Dreamer's loss, even if it does not offer obvious consolation or resolve itself the way classical dialogues usually do. The problems and tensions inherent in these disparate literary traditions are made self-consciously explicit in the poem, which begins as a dream vision and moves toward Christian revelation. The Dreamer is confused about where he is in his dream and about whether the Pearl Maiden is physically there where he sees her, and when he wakes up, he wonders whether what he has learned has been a "ueray and soth sermoun" (1185; a really true lesson).

In one important respect, however, *Pearl* is not like most late medieval dream visions, whether romantic, social, philosophical, or religious, for it is not a personification allegory.[8] That many elements within the dream in *Pearl* are not what they seem to human senses is unquestionably true, but most of us do not consider *Pearl* an allegory in the ways in which *The Romance of the Rose* or *Piers Plowman* is. In *Pearl* there is no figure comparable to Idleness, who opens the door to the Garden of Love for the Lover in *The Romance of the Rose,* nor is the young woman who instructs the Dreamer in *Pearl* given an abstract name like Philosophia, the figure who guides Boethius in the *Consolation of Philosophy,* or Reason, who tries to enlighten the Lover in *The Romance of the Rose.* In *Pearl* the maiden is called "Pearl" (actually, and this is critical, the Dreamer calls her "my pearl" throughout the poem), and whatever a pearl is, it is not an abstraction, but a concrete thing, which may (and almost certainly does) symbolize something else or, as I believe, some *things* else. Boethius's Philosophia represents the wisdom and knowledge of Neoplatonic philosophy—in other words, Philosophia is philosophy— but to understand what the Pearl represents we must move from the sign of "pearl" (as word and as thing) to something else, which is not given a name or a title within the poem. Thus, we are in a world of sym-

bols, like the cross or the pentangle, not in a world of allegorical person-
ifications.

To say that the Pearl is a pearl (as Philosophia is philosophy) and that
the Dreamer lost this pearl is where we begin, but we then must read
the poem to learn who and what that pearl is—we cannot immediately
recognize her as we do Reason in *The Romance of the Rose* or Patience in
Piers Plowman. Furthermore, the pearl does not have one meaning, nor is
it one thing. Rather, there are many pearls: the pearl the Dreamer lost
before the dream "in on erbere; / Þurȝ gresse to grounde" (9–10; in a
garden of herbs, through grass to ground); the Pearl Maiden the
Dreamer encounters within the dream; the pearls that bedeck the
crowns and breasts of the Pearl Maiden and her fellow maidens; the pearl
that the narrator commends to Christ after the dream; the pearls that
the poet prays we all can become in heaven; and finally the pearl that is
the poem. The connections between the various pearls that appear or are
mentioned in the poem—how they are related, how one becomes another—these are what the poem is about. How these connections are made
is what the poem does—it is part of the story of the poem.

The Story of *Pearl*

To understand the meaning and the identity of the pearl and the subject of the dream and the poem, we need to take a closer and more
detailed look at the poem's "plot," next to identify and characterize the
versification, and then to consider some of its complex language games,
drawing on the poet's literary, biblical, and exegetical sources when necessary, but focusing on what the poem tells us about itself, its subject,
and in particular about pearl(s). The story told in *Pearl,* as I summarized
it in the opening paragraph of this chapter, seems simple enough.
However, once one begins to detail the events and figures of the poem,
interpretation plays a part and each of us will recount a slightly different
version of what happens. What follows is what I believe "happens" in
the poem.

The narrator, after opening with an emotional stanza that praises his
pearl and laments her loss (in the present tense), then moves on to his
account (in the past tense) of a past experience. One day, he tells us, he
is grieving over his pearl in a garden and falls asleep. While asleep, he
dreams of being in a beautiful garden, through which he wanders filled
with desire, until he comes to a stream and across the stream sees a
young girl. Frozen in fear and joy, he gazes upon this figure, who is

dressed in white and bedecked with pearls, with a crown of pearls on her head, and "a wonder perle withouten wemme" (221; a wondrous, perfect pearl) set in her breast. The narrator greets the maiden, asking if she is truly his pearl whom he has lost: "Art þou my perle þat I haf playned?" (242; Art thou my pearl that I have grieved for?), the pearl that left him a "joylez juelere" (251; joyless jeweller). She answers that she is and immediately begins to scold him for failing to be a "kynde" (276; good and true, because natural), or a "gentyl" (264; noble) jeweller.

The Dreamer and the Maiden continue talking for most of the remainder of the poem. Actually, the Maiden does most of the talking, for her role is clearly that of an authority figure, instructing her wrong-thinking and often irrational pupil. It becomes clear from the first exchanges and subsequent details that the pearl the Dreamer has lost was in his waking life a very young girl, who "lyfed not two ȝer in oure þede" (483; lived not even two full years in this world). Presumably, she was the narrator's daughter, since he has told us earlier: "ho watz nerre þen aunte or nece" (233; she was closer to me than an aunt or niece).[9] The Pearl Maiden goes on to tell the Dreamer that she is in another world now, and that she lives a blissful life as a queen in heaven married to the Lamb.

Then follows the debate proper, in which the Dreamer questions how the Pearl Maiden can be a queen when there is only one Queen of Heaven—Mary—and how the Maiden can be saved when she was not even old enough to know her prayers when she died (485). The Pearl Maiden answers the Dreamer by retelling the Parable of the Vineyard, and expanding upon it and explicating it much in the manner of a biblical exegete. The parable is about a vineyard owner who hires workers throughout the course of the day to labor in his vineyard and then at the end of the day pays them all the same wage, no matter whether they have been working since early morning or only for a few hours. The story illustrates the paradox of divine justice, which does not conform with human standards and values, for divine justice, as the Dreamer protests to his teacher, is "unreasonable" to his way of thinking (590).

The dialogue continues, moving from this question of divine justice to the nature of salvation itself: what heaven is like, what precisely marriage to the Lamb is like. The Pearl Maiden uses John's Apocalypse to describe the bliss of the 144,000, who live and celebrate their joy in the New Jerusalem. The Dreamer keeps confusing the earthly with the divine: because he judges divine justice by human values, so he thinks the New Jerusalem is the same as the historical Jerusalem, which is in

Judea (922). In her instruction the Pearl Maiden continues to quote and
paraphrase biblical and exegetical sources, especially the Apocalypse.

The debate draws to an end, without much indication that the
Dreamer has come round to his teacher's point of view, although his
questions indicate that at least he accepts the reality that she indeed lives
in another world. The Dreamer then asks to be brought to the Pearl
Maiden's home. This he is denied, but he is told that the Lamb has
granted that the Dreamer may be given "a syȝt þerof" (968; a vision
thereof). The dream climaxes in a vision of the New Jerusalem, of the
Lamb, and of the 144,000 singing the Lamb's praises. All of the descriptive details of this vision come (as the narrator reminds us many times)
directly from the visions recounted in the Apocalypse: "As deuysez hit þe
apostel John" (984; as John the Apostle set it down). The Dreamer then
is seized with "luf-longyng" (1152; desire) at the sight of what he calls
"*my* lyttel quene" (1147; *my* little queen—emphasis mine); he tries to
cross the stream to her; and the dream abruptly ends.

When he awakens in the garden, the Dreamer is overcome with
anguish and remorse at his rashness, which has brought the dream to an
end. He then meditates briefly on his "avysyoun" (1184; vision) and
thinks that if the lessons he was told are true, if she really dwells in
heaven, then he is resigned to his situation, namely "þys doel-doun-
goun" (1187; this dungeon of woe). For some of us the qualification of
the "if clause" is important for this poem, which never reaches the kind
of certainty found in many visions of the otherworld, whether pagan or
Christian. However, the Dreamer's resignation does become stronger a
little later, in the last stanza. There the poem moves back into the present tense of the frame, with the narrator commenting that he has since
commended the pearl to Christ and that he has found Christ, who is
revealed in the Eucharist, to be "a God, a Lorde, a frende ful fyin"
(1204; a God, a Lord, a friend most noble). Following this commenda-
tion, the poem concludes with a prayer that the Dreamer and his fellows (he uses the first-person *plural* for the first time) be brought to the
same bliss the pearl enjoys, the joy of being part of God's household:
"He gef vus to be His homly hyne / Ande precious perlez vnto His pay"
(1211–12; May he grant us to be his household servants and precious
pearls for his pleasure).[10]

Much is missing from this summary of the poem's story, of course.
Certain readers would insist that what is most missing is the theological
and philosophical background—the medieval views on salvation, in particular—but I do not think such is the case. It is certainly helpful to have

a general understanding of the medieval Christian's worldview, especially the conviction shared by even the most "worldly" of poets like Chaucer, that the things of this world—money, fame, and even human feelings and human love—finally do not matter. Also, some specific details, like the Dreamer's concern because the Pearl Maiden did not have the chance to learn her prayers before she died, require a bit of explanation for most modern readers. Still, the general intellectual climate of the poem is not especially arcane or complicated. The poem, in fact, works on the assumption that the Dreamer, and by extension every reader with the Dreamer's same weaknesses and needs, is not a theologian nor a philosopher, but instead an ordinary Christian who has a problem and who has gotten a few things wrong. (In this respect, *Pearl* is quite different from Boethius's *Consolation of Philosophy,* since in that work the dreamer is identified as a philosopher, and his guide works to remind him of the philosophical principles he once knew and has since forgotten.) Any good annotated edition or translation should supply readers with the information they need to follow the debate between the Pearl Maiden and the Dreamer; in fact, a bit of ignorance about late medieval thought can be an asset, since it places the reader in much the same position as the Dreamer, who seems to be quite poorly schooled in the theology of salvation.

Far more than intellectual background, what is most missing from the preceding summary of *Pearl* are the versification and the language play, for so much of the development, so much of what "happens" in the poem, depends upon poetic craft. The poem's medium is very much a part of its message, and like most good lyric poems, and more than many longer medieval texts, the form of *Pearl* is inextricably bound up with its content. We need, then, to examine the technical aspects of the poem and its language before we try to answer some of the critical issues, such as what the pearl is, or what the pearls are, and what happens to the Dreamer by the end of the poem.

The Language and Versification of *Pearl*

While *Pearl* uses the alliterative line, its verse is the least typical alliterative verse of all the Pearl poet's works. The most striking features of *Pearl*'s verse, in fact, are wholly uncharacteristic of alliterative poetry. *Pearl*'s verse unit is a 12-line stanza, rhyming *abab abab bcbc.* Here is a typical stanza, with the *a* rhymes underlined, the *b* rhymes italicized, and the *c* rhymes in bold:

"Cortayse quen," þenne sayde þat <u>gaye</u>,
Knelande to grounde, folde vp hyr *face*,
"Makelez moder and myryest <u>may</u>,
Blessed bygynner of vch a *grace*!"
Þenne ros ho vp and con <u>restay</u>,
And speke me towarde in þat *space*:
"Sir, fele her porchasez and fongez <u>pray</u>,
Bot supplantorez none withinne þys *place*;
Þat emperise al heuenz *hatz*—
And vrþe and helle—in her **bayly**;
Of erytage ȝet non wyl ho *chace*,
For ho is quen of **cortaysye**."
(433–44; emphasis mine)[11]

"Courteous Queen!" that blithe one <u>said</u>
Kneeling to ground with upturned *face*,
"Matchless Mother, most lovely <u>Maid</u>,
Blessed beginner of every *grace*!"
Then rose she up, and silent <u>stayed</u>,
And spoke to me across that *space*:
"Sir, gifts are gained here, and prizes <u>paid</u>,
But none on another presumes or *preys*.
Empress peerless ever to *praise*
Of heaven and earth and hell is **she**,
Yet puts no man from his rightful *place*,
For she is Queen of **courtesy**.
(Borroff trans.; emphasis mine)

Within the stanzas, as the way I have written the rhyme scheme indicates, the lines group themselves by sound into three quatrains (which, as in the above example, the syntax and sense usually observes), the last quatrain at once joined to the first two by its *b* rhyme, but signaling the end of the stanza with the new *c* rhyme. In this particular stanza the last quatrain summarizes and emphasizes the point made in the first two quatrains: that Mary, the Empress of Heaven, is supreme, but since she is Queen of Courtesy she does not supplant any other queen—this is a typically paradoxical, even oxymoronic, statement about the rewards of heaven, a way of saying all who dwell there are equal and uncompetitive, but that one is more equal than others, without competing.

These 12-line stanzas are arranged into groups of five, which make up 20 sections in the poem (for a total of 101 stanzas, because one section has six stanzas, of which more later). These sections are marked in the manuscript by illuminated capitals;[12] and, within a given section, the stanzas are joined by *concatenation*, the repetition of a word or phrase in the first and last lines of each stanza within a section. For example, in section 3 the linking phrase is "more and more"; here are the second and third stanzas of that section:

> More of wele watz in þat wyse
> Þen I cowþe telle þaȝ I tom hade,
> For vrþely herte myȝt not suffyse
> To þe tenþe dole of þo gladnez glade.
> Forþy I þoȝt þat paradyse
> Watz þer ouer gayn þo bonkez brade;
> I hope þe water were a deuyse
> Bytwene myrþez by merez made;
> Byȝonde þe broke, by slente oþer slade,
> I hoped þat mote merked wore.
> Bot þe water watz depe, I dorst not wade,
> And euer me longed ay more and more.
>
> More and more, and ȝet wel mare,
> Me lyste to se þe broke byȝonde,
> For if hit watz fayr þer I con fare,
> Wel loueloker watz þe fyrre londe.
> Abowte me con I stote and stare;
> To fynde a forþe faste con I fonde,
> Bot woþez mo iwysse þer ware,
> Þe fyrre I stalked by þe stronde;
> And euer me þoȝt I schulde not wonde
> For wo þer welez so wynne wore.
> Þenne nwe note me com on honde"

Þat meued my mynde ay <u>more and more</u>.
                    (133–56; emphasis mine)

<u>More</u> of bliss was there to prize
Than ever my tongue could testify,
For earthly heart could not suffice
To sustain one tenth of that pure joy.
It could not be but Paradise
Lay beyond those noble banks, thought I,
And the stream itself seemed a device,
A mark to know a boundary by.
Those peerless precincts to espy
I need but gain the further shore;
But I dared not wade, for the water ran high,
And longing mastered me <u>more and more</u>.

<u>More</u> than ever and ever the <u>more</u>
To cross that river was all my care,
For lovely though this landscape were,
What lay beyond was past compare.
I stared about, scanning the shore
For a ford to afford me thoroughfare,
But dangers direr than before
Appeared, the more I wandered there.
And still it seemed I should not forbear
For dangers, with delights in store;
But now was broached a new affair
My mind was moved by,<u> more and more</u>.
                    (Borroff trans.; emphasis mine)

The variation of the linking phrase, "more and more," in the above example—using "more" in the first line in some cases, and both "more and more" and "mare" (here spelled with an "a") in one case—is typical. Usually the phrase is more constant in the last lines than in the first ones, and sometimes the linking word or phrase does not appear in the first line at all; this allows the poet a little more leeway, although the demands of the concatenation are still heavy.

The alliteration of this verse is often reduced, and in many lines the caesura is barely observed in syntax or sense. For example, in the sample stanzas given above, many lines alliterate only two stresses. In the first of the two stanzas no lines alliterate all four stresses. (Recall that three is the usual number of alliterating stresses, in both Old English and Middle English poetry, but that Middle English, unlike Old English, frequently alliterates all four stressed syllables.) However, in the second of the quoted stanzas, there are two lines (150, 154) that alliterate all four stresses, while one line (156), the last of the stanza, is hypermetric, with five alliterating and stressed syllables. (Some might not give full stress to the extra alliterating syllable "my," although I believe it is nearly impossible to read the line without according this word at least secondary stress.) This extra alliteration works here to add emotional intensity, in keeping with the sense of the stanza, which describes the Dreamer's increasing, almost frantic, longing to cross the river. It also prepares us for the climactic moment in the next stanza, when he first catches sight of the Maiden: "a faunt, / A mayden of menske, ful debonere" (161–62; a child, an honorable maiden, very gracious). Generally, however, the poet avoids extra alliteration, and the rhyme scheme of *Pearl* is usually strong enough to prevail over the sound impression of the alliteration.

Furthermore, the meter is actually quite irregular, in the sense that there is no consistent pattern of the relationship of unstressed to stressed, no regular scheme of rising or falling feet ("rising" describes feet that begin with unstressed syllable[s] and end, or "rise" up, to stressed ones). Since there is less regularity in the meter, the effect of the stress, already decreased by the limited alliteration, is further weakened. In addition, the poet does not usually emphasize the caesura: the sense and syntax often carry across from the first half-line to the second, and not infrequently a scheme of paired alliteration joins the two half-lines. For example, in the passage quoted above, the line, "Bot þe *w*ater watz *d*epe, I *d*orst not *w*ade," pairs the alliterating sounds of *w* and *d*; effectively, this bridges the caesura, which here is otherwise emphasized by the syntax. All of these modifications of the traditional alliterative line serve, I believe, to draw greater attention to the rhyme.

Obviously, this rhyme and stanza scheme places great demands on the poet. The complex versification of *Pearl* is important, even to readers who can only know the poem in translation, because it is an integral part of what the poem is, what it does, and what it is about. No poem written in such a demanding verse form can fail to draw attention to itself, saying as it were: "Look at me! Isn't this brilliant!" The values implicit in such self-consciousness are important; the clear implication is that the formal and the elegant and the clever are good and beautiful. There are no "diamonds in the rough" here, but instead (to use the poem's own phrases) a "precios perle wythouten spotte" (36; a precious pearl without a blemish) and "to clanly clos in golde so clere" (2; perfectly set in shining gold).[13] Furthermore, the poet who crafts the poem takes obvious pride and care in the making of his poem. He is, again to use the poem's terms, the Jeweller, so named by himself and the Pearl Maiden early in their conversation (252, 264); and he sees his task is to set his poem "sengeley in synglure" (8; singly, or uniquely, in singular, or by itself). As the Jeweller's problem and feelings are explicitly the subject of the poem, at least at first, so too his behavior, his skills and craft, are implicitly at the poem's center, at least until the vision. This is the main reason for avoiding an overly simplistic dichotomy between poet and narrator, for much of the poem's effect depends upon our human inclination to identify the narrator with the poet. We need to understand that the Jeweller is not just the first-person narrator lamenting his pearl, or the Dreamer who meets the Pearl Maiden and is shown a vision of the New Jerusalem, but also the poet who crafts the poem that records those experiences. There is, of course, a tension created by the differences in the Jeweller's several perspectives, differences that arise partly from shifts in time and partly from shifts in mode. From the perspective of the poet who crafts his poem after the dream, the Jeweller is able to view his grieving and lamenting self with a point of view closer to that of the Pearl Maiden's. In particular, the larger perspective of the poet comes to be less self-absorbed and less possessive about his pearl and its setting than the Dreamer's view is within the dream. For the poet's evolved sense of the pearl includes some of what he learns from the Pearl Maiden, who discusses salvation and heaven for everyone (not just for herself and her Jeweller). Furthermore, thanks to the Pearl Maiden, the poet learns that there is a jeweller far more skillful than he, one who makes the true and perfect setting for the pearl, indeed for all pearls.

Wordplay in *Pearl*

In addition to the versification, other aspects of the poem's language, in particular its virtuoso wordplay, help characterize the Jeweller as a highly skilled and self-conscious poet. However, much of the poem's

wordplay is more properly the Pearl Maiden's, who uses a kind of punning, combined with definition and explication (and a bit of implicit ety-
mology), as a central part of her teaching. Whether directly quoted from
the Pearl Maiden, or indirectly based on biblical sources, or the Jeweller's
own descriptions of his waking and dream experiences, the poem's wordplay focuses on the linking words. These words, in turn, thus serve several functions in the poem: they join the stanzas within sections; they
outline the Dreamer's experience thematically and linguistically; they
provide a kind of verbal summary of the Pearl Maiden's teaching and the
vision's revelation; and, through these several ways, the linking words
serve the additional function of unifying the poem and outlining its
development.

As examples of the Jeweller's verbal craft, we can take two different
series, one from the beginning of the poem and therefore primarily from
the Jeweller's personal perspective, and one toward the end that enjoys
the larger vision gained through the dream. The linking words of the first
five sections of the poem are, respectively: "precios [or priuy] perle withouten spot" (precious/own pearl without blemish); "adubbemente"
(adornment); "more and more"; "perlez pyʒte" (pearls placed, that is, as
decoration); and "jueler" (jeweller). These early phrases, all belonging to
the mode of lyric love poetry, emphasize beauty and desire. Their
sequence shows the Dreamer's movement: from lamenting his own lost
"precious pearl" outside the dream, to the "adornment" of the dream garden, which stirs his desire "more and more," until he comes upon his
transformed pearl, adorned with "precious pearls" (no longer his own
"privy perle"). The sequence then ends with the narrator's identification
as a "jeweller," the poet/lover who admires jewels and sets them in poetry.

In the vision of the heavenly city that climaxes the dream (sections 17
through 19), the linking words point to revelatory vision. The vision of
the "Apostle John" (the linking phrase of section 17) is of the New
Jerusalem, a world of light beyond this sublunary world ("anvnder mone"
[under moon] in section 18), a city of "gret delyt" (great joy, the linking
phrase for section 19) for the blessed who sing the Lamb's praises.

Sometimes the linking words and some of the wordplay seem
strained, especially to moderns. The phrase "anvnder mone" is one
example of the poet's overreaching. To appreciate this term, it helps to
have a sense of medieval cosmology, to know that for the people of the
Middle Ages the earth lay at the center of the universe and was separated from the heavenly spheres by the moon and the lunar sphere and that
all below was transitory and all above eternal. Even so, "anvnder mone"

seems a farfetched term to feature in a heavenly vision (to emphasize the differences between heaven and earth it would be clearer and simpler to use the word "earth" or a synonym). A clue that perhaps the poet was less than comfortable with the phrase is that it is used least consistently and with the most variations of any of the linking phrases: the first lines use only "mone" or "sunne ne mone" (neither sun nor moon); and the last lines have "sunne ne mone" (1044), "sunne and mone" (1055), "anvnder mone" (1068, 1092; under moon) and "vche a mone" (1080; every moon). A partial reason for the variation and the choice of the word "mone" would be that it is not just the sublunary transitory nature of the moon that is indicated, but its inadequate light, its dimness beside the Lamb, for the Lamb is the lamp (the poem insists on the "Lamb/lamp" pun) that sheds the ultimate light. This said, one still feels a strain in the attempt to say so much and relate so many points with one short phrase.[14] This feeling of strain, as well as the sense of preciousness and self-conscious crafting that arises from *Pearl*'s intricate verse form, is a valid and important response to the poem. Like the artificiality of the dream garden, with its gems and "unnatural" precious materials, the poem is not naturally beautiful—it is unnaturally beautiful, artfully and, even artificially, crafted.

While the Jeweller's versification and concatenation can seem farfetched or even overly precious, the wordplay used by the Pearl Maiden in her dialogue with the Dreamer presents a somewhat different kind of difficulty. At once more learned and more playful, the Pearl Maiden's wordplay places tough intellectual demands upon the reader, while also challenging logical and informed thinking. Her wordplay begins with scholarly, written exegesis on the written word, but works from this basis to a freedom from human language, partly by expanding the meanings of words and partly by exploiting their contradictions. Especially revealing in this regard is the Pearl Maiden's discussion of the Parable of the Vineyard in sections 9 through 11, at which I would like now to take a closer look. Serving both the reader and the Dreamer as a verbal introduction and preparation for the vision of the New Jerusalem, the Pearl Maiden's lesson of the parable forms the structural and thematic center of the poem.[15] As used by the Pearl Maiden, the link words of these middle sections——"date," "more," and "gret inoghe," respectively—define and describe heavenly reward, so different from its counterparts on earth.

"Date," like its modern equivalent *date,* points to the limits and finiteness of earthly time, thereby drawing attention to the eschaton, the end of time when Jesus will return for the Second Coming and will call all to the Last Judgment. The working day in the vineyard, like human life on earth, like the created world itself, is specific and finite—the day's end, and earthly time's end, looms over all. The vineyard owner says to the workers: "Why stande ȝe ydel? . . . Ne knawe ȝe of þis day no *date?*" (515–16; emphasis mine; Why do you stand around idle? . . . Don't you realize what *time of day* it is?). Later, when the vineyard owner brings more workers in, the narrator comments that "Welneȝ wyl *day* watz passed *date*" (528; emphasis mine; the *day* had almost reached its *end*).

"Date," as the Pearl Maiden uses it in this section, refers not just to limits in time, but also to limits in happiness and reward. "Date" is the reward enjoyed by the Pearl Maiden, a reward that is too high a rank, according to the Jeweller, who cries: "Bot a quene!—hit is to dere a *date*" (492; emphasis mine; But a queen—that is too great a *reward*)[16] This latter use of "date" is different from ours today and apparently also from the more common uses in the fourteenth century, since there is no other recorded instance of the word that would help translate it in the sense in which it seems to be used in this line.[17]

What the Pearl Maiden is doing with the word "date" here is typical: she takes its common meaning, a specific time, expands it to a less common one—"date" as the end of a period of time—and then pushes it to refer (almost figuratively) to any limit, not just a limit in time. In the poem's uses, "date," as a human term and concept, tells us something about the finiteness of our earthly life, but it is inappropriate for divine justice. As the Pearl tells the Dreamer: "Þer is no *date* of Hys godnesse" (493; emphasis mine; There is no *limit* to His [God's] goodness). In other words, the word "date" refers both to the limit that restricts our time on earth and also to the limit that does not restrict God. The pun on "date" thus teaches the same lessons as the parable: on the one hand, time is limited and the end is coming, so God's laborers must work hard to earn their reward; on the other hand, there is no limit to God's goodness, and his divine justice is not constrained by human values.

A similar point is made by the linking words of the following sections: "more" and "gret innoȝe." "More" is primarily a human term, one that signals human desire and is associated with *cupiditas*. Cupiditas is literally the sin of greed, especially material greed, but in the medieval worldview cupiditas is not confined to material greed: it also embraces the love and desire for all worldly things, not just wealth or fame, but anything of this world, including other humans. To many theologians, cupiditas is the ultimate sin, because it draws God's people away from him. Cupiditas is opposed to *caritas,* the love of God that includes love of his other creatures. Loving one's fellows is good—it is caritas or divine love—if one loves *because of* God; but if one loves another *instead of* God (which is what lust is), then it is cupiditas or worldly love. Cupiditas is unsatisfying and characterized by a greed for more, like sexual desire or worldly ambition. Caritas, in contrast, satisfies because it is divine and therefore complete.

Cupiditas seems to be the kind of desire implied in "more and more," the linking phrase of section 3, where the Dreamer responds with delight to the love garden of his dream and speaks of a very human longing to increase that pleasure. In section 10, which retells the Parable of the Vineyard, "more" refers to another kind of cupiditas, the ambition for material reward and particularly for receiving more payment than one's fellows, but since the parable is about salvation, this ambition becomes in fact the greed for a greater heavenly reward. Both of these kinds of desire, one experienced by the Dreamer and one by the workers in the parable, are wrong, for the point of the parable is that heavenly rewards do not work according to human desire and ambition. The dissatisfaction and frustration implied in any human desire are inappropriate when speaking of heaven.

As the linking phrase of section 11 puts it: "For þe grace of God is gret inoghe" (610, 624, 636, 660; for the grace of God is great enough)—desire for "more" is overcome by the unlimited sufficiency of divine grace. However, after setting up this dichotomy between desire and satisfaction, between "more" and "gret inoghe," and ruling completely in favor of sufficiency, the Pearl poet then undercuts the lesson with a typical bit of linguistic paradox. For in this section, and in no other, the linking phrase is an entire line, repeated verbatim at the end of every stanza except one, in which "wex" (grows) replaces "is"—a case of substituting "becoming" for "being" (648). By this ploy the Pearl Maiden draws attention to the paradox of sufficiency in increasing abundance; for, having repeated that grace is enough, she now insists (in the second-to-last stanza of the section) that the grace will grow to be enough. Furthermore, since this variation concludes the stanza that describes the saving actions of Christ's Passion, the Pearl poet is able to have it both ways: God's mercy is always sufficient, but, with the historical events of Christ's life, it has become, in time, more sufficient (a contradiction in terms, of course).

Another bit of wordplay involves the same paradox of sufficiency in increasing abundance. The closing line of section 10 reads: "And euer þe lenger the lasse þe more" (600). Translated, this line does not make a lot of sense; some possibilities are: "And increasingly, the less [they do], the more [they receive]" (Vantuono, ed.); or, better: "However much less so much the more" (Andrew and Waldron, eds.). Cawley and Anderson, like Vantuono, translate the line so that it specifically refers to the laborers' work—and it does indeed complete the preceding line, "Þenne the lasse in werke to take more able" (599; then those who did less work were able to get more). However, such a reading ignores the fact that the latter line's ellipsis of all references to agents or actions allows it to become more abstract and to refer simultaneously to both the literal story of a vineyard and also to the figurative story of salvation. (This way of exploiting the inherent ambiguity of his syntax and verse is very characteristic of the poet; he does it often with the short lines [called "bobs"] in *Gawain*.) What is striking, moreover, is that "more," the human word and the concept, is now used for divine reward. Through wordplay and paradox, "more" has been transformed from *cupiditas* to *caritas*, from human desire to divine love and mercy.

The poem continues to work with this same kind of punning paradox in the next section in which the Pearl Maiden explains that God's kingdom is both "more" and "lasse"—it is sufficient.[18] Later, in section 15, which is the section with six stanzas instead of five, the paradox reaches a point where it is actually played out in the versification. Significantly, the linking word in section 15 is "neuerþelesse" (852, 864, 876, 888, 900, 912). The term means essentially what it does in modern English ("even so" or "notwithstanding"), but the poet has exploited its inherent paradox, namely, that it works as an absolute ("always the same"), while incorporating a comparative form ("less"). In other words, in section 15, the lesson is that the Lamb's reward for all his brides is the same perfect and unvarying bliss, literally beyond comparison, and yet the Pearl Maiden uses comparison when she says it is "never any *less*" (emphasis mine). Furthermore, the section has "more" stanzas than any other, even as it insists on the fullness of sufficiency. One effect of this punning paradox is to remind us that human forms and human language must resort to comparison because our world is one of incompleteness, where there always is more to be desired. God can use the perfection of a circle, for example, or of a perfect number like 100, but humans are inclined to push for "more than perfect" and to give the circle an extra bump, or to add one more to 100, as the poet does when he adds the sixth stanza to section 15, and brings the poem's total number to 101.

The Jeweller

The elaborate wordplay and tour-de-force rhetorical structuring, which are such important parts of the Pearl Maiden's lesson, lead up to her announcement to the Jeweller that it has been granted to him to see the heavenly city. Thus the verbal has introduced the visual, but introduced it not so much by reason and logical argument as by challenging and stretching the Dreamer's earthbound assumptions with startling and unusual uses of language, thus preparing him for a heavenly vision.

Since the Pearl Maiden's verbal instruction is followed by the vision of the New Jerusalem, which she says has been granted to the Jeweller, it would appear that he has merited this vision, presumably because he has profited from the Pearl Maiden's lesson. There is definitely a progressive revelation in the dream: from the verbal, exegetical discourse on the Parable of the Vineyard; next to the Pearl-Maiden's description of the New Jerusalem, which is equally elaborate in wordplay, but much more visual than the exegesis of the markedly non-visual parable; and finally to the vision itself. However, the Pearl Maiden never says the vision is a reward, only that she has received a "great favor" from the Lamb: "Bot of þe Lombe I haue þe aquylde / For a syȝt þerof þurȝ gret fauor" (967–68; But from the Lamb, as a great favor, I have obtained permission for a vision for you). If anything, it would seem that the Pearl Maiden acquired this favor even before she first appeared to the Jeweller (although it is perhaps inappropriate to apply temporal sequentiality to a dream).

In trying to follow the Jeweller's progress, or lack thereof, we need to distinguish between his development and the poem's. Although the dream moves forward in its revelations, there is little suggestion that the Jeweller himself progresses from his earthbound self to enlightenment. Some mistakes he does correct. For example, he apologizes for blaming "Wyrde" (fate) for his loss, and he stops thinking that just because he "sees" the Pearl Maiden across the river that she is really in that place, an assumption that proves, as she says, that "Þy word byfore þy wytte con fle" (294; your words run ahead of your sense). Shortly thereafter, when the Jeweller in effect acknowledges his stupid blundering, explaining that he is "bot mol and manerez mysse" (382; mere dirt and lacking in any manners), the Pearl Maiden tells him that his speech is now pleasing to her (400), for her Lord likes meekness and hates willful pride. So the Jeweller does learn something, and he does move from the bitter grief of his waking world, to his humble pleasure in the Pearl Maiden's lessons, and later to the bliss of seeing her among the 144,000. Yet most of the progress in the dream is not earned by the Jeweller. It is not internalized; in other words, we do not see him change his heart or his thinking—we only observe that his manners and speech change. In fact, it is precisely the Jeweller's change in "speech" that the Pearl Maiden tells him she likes.

Moreover, there is much evidence that at the end of his dream the Jeweller is as burdened by his mortal longing, his selfish desire, his will-fulness, and his inability to distinguish heavenly from earthly as he was at the beginning of the dream. His limited understanding of God's king-dom and of those who enjoy it is betrayed in several ways, both before the vision and during it. The Jeweller's human selfishness (his *cupiditas*), which seems to be repressed for a time during the Pearl Maiden's teach-ing, returns with such force during the vision that it causes the abrupt end to the dream.

Some of the Jeweller's misunderstandings seem quite stupid, even laughable. One of the most persistent, his failure to distinguish earthly places from heavenly, is part of his inability to understand that God's kingdom is not bound by finite dimensions of space and time. Just before the dream's visionary climax, despite the Jeweller's apparent acknowledgment that the Pearl is not in the place ("mote") where he sees her, the Jeweller still wonders where she lives, that is, what place ("mote"), bounded by a moat (also "mote"), she and her fellow maidens inhabit. Endearingly but foolishly, the Jeweller exclaims: "So cumly a pakke of joly juele / Wer euel don schulde ly3 þeroute" (929–30; For so comely a pack of pretty jewels, it would be a terrible thing if they were to have to stay outdoors). Similarly, the Jeweller has first thought that the Jerusalem the Pearl has been describing is in Judea, and even after she explains that there are two Jerusalems—an earthly one and a heav-enly one—and that she and her fellow queens live in the heavenly one, a spot without a spot ("moteless mote"), still the Jeweller thinks of it as a place, a defined physical spot, to which he asks her to lead him (936).

A more serious error in the Jeweller's understanding comes during the vision, when he fails to recognize or understand the Lamb's wounds. When he sees the Lamb, the narrator's description focuses first on the glory of the Lamb and his followers, his "meyny schene" (1145; splendid company), which includes the procession of the 144,000 and the elders and angels who surround the throne and sing praises to the Lamb (1096–1126). The "great delight" that fills this company and is "caught" by the Jeweller is interrupted midstanza when he sees the Lamb's wound, so huge and bloody (1135). The Jeweller's reaction betrays not just his appropriate sorrow over the Lamb's pain, but also his totally inappropriate ignorance about the Crucifixion: "Alas, þoȝt I, who did þat spyt?" (1138; Alas, thought I, who did that terrible deed?). This is not the first reference to the Crucifixion, for before this the Pearl Maiden has referred several times to Christ's Passion. In section 14, in which the linking word is "Jerusalem," the Pearl Maiden describes at length Christ's suffering in Jerusalem and compares him to a lamb led to the slaughter. Again, in section 16, when correcting the Jeweller's confusion regarding the two Jerusalems, the Pearl Maiden identifies the earthly Jerusalem as the one where the Lamb chose to suffer in order to ensure our peace—a pun on one traditional, supposedly etymological, definition of Jerusalem as a "vision of peace" (Andrew and Waldron, eds., 99, note to lines 949–56).

The basic truths concerning the Crucifixion and its saving grace are probably the most central ones of Christianity. The Jeweller should know them without being told, but to be told and still appear ignorant about the Lamb's wound during the vision is to be the kind of hopelessly dense and inattentive student all teachers dread. It could be said that the Jeweller's ignorance is a kind of ploy that allows him to express fresh sorrow over the Lamb's suffering and to ask who did that terrible thing. (The answer, of course, is that everyone, including the Jeweller, did.) However, while the Jeweller's ignorance about the Lamb's wound may serve an expressive purpose in the poem, it still undermines the probability that his understanding of Christian truths has earned him a vision.

Moreover, the Jeweller's pity for Christ's suffering does not have the proper effect. Such pity is often deliberately aroused in late medieval art, in sermons, prayers, and hymns, as well as in plays, poetry, and treatises on sin. This aroused pity is meant to move sinners to repent and mend their ways. But this is precisely what does not happen to the Jeweller in *Pearl* when he sees the Lamb's wound. In fact, the Jeweller's horror, ignorant but expressive, is immediately followed by a stanza that shows him as willful, as selfish, and as filled with "luf-longyng" (desire) as he is before the dream begins.[19]

The stanza that follows the one describing the Lamb's wound is the stanza in which the Jeweller sees the Pearl Maiden among her "ferez" (1150; fellows), the "meyny schene" (1145; the shining company). The sight of her, whom he calls "*my* lyttel quene" (1147; emphasis mine; *my* little queen), fills him with "luf-longyng" and that desire melts him to madness (1154), a madness characterized by foolish, self-centered willfulness: "Quen *I* seȝ *my* frely, *I wolde* be þere, / Byȝonde þe water þaȝ ho were walte" (1155–56; emphasis mine; When *I* saw *my* gracious one, *I willed* to be there). Driven by his desire, the Jeweller plunges into the river and is instantly flung out of his dream. This kind of desire, this passion that conquers reason, is familiar from medieval love poetry (and much love poetry and song ever since), and although it was common then and since to describe divine love (God's love for humanity and hopefully theirs for him) in terms of the powerful feelings of romantic love, nothing about the Jeweller's "luf-longyng" is divine—it is human *cupiditas*. The Jeweller's desire for *his* pearl (the possessive is completely wrong) and his unconverted will dominate the poetry, for the first-person singular is pervasive in these lines, as it is at the beginning of the poem. As the Jeweller later admits, all of this is against God's will or the "Pryncez paye" (1164; Prince's pleasure).

The Jeweller, of course, realizes his mistake immediately and regrets it, but even his regret is excessive, at least at first. He tells of his anguish, when he awakened in "gret affray" (great dismay) and "raxled" (1174)—the Middle English word *raxled* is a wonderful bit of onomatopoeia, describing and sounding like a kind of wrenching movement. This heavy regret gradually gives way to a calmer resignation, in which the Jeweller does seem to have reached some kind of consolation: at least he gains the ability to evaluate his behavior and to find it wanting. However, the consolation is qualified and more forced upon him by his rash and willful act than gradually acquired by the Pearl Maiden's careful teaching or even by the divinely granted vision.

The final stanza of the poem represents the strongest and most dramatic change in the Jeweller's attitude. In these closing lines he commends his pearl to God and finally lets go of his obsessive possessiveness. Even more significantly, for the first time he moves from the first-person singular to the first-person plural. His prayer that God grant *us* to be his followers is caritas at last. It is important, I believe, that this stanza is the final one, and that moreover it is in a different mode and mood from all that precedes it. The poem has included, in the opening stanzas, the present tense of present sorrow and the past tense of grief and regret, followed by the dream mode in which moods and attitudes change quickly and not always logically. With the final stanza, the poet once again uses the present and present perfect tenses, but it is a present of resignation and hope, in contrast to the present mood of grief that opens the poem. However, we have no reason to believe that the first present, when the Jeweller watches and waits longingly in the garden, is any less "present" than the closing mood, no logical reason, that is, beyond the fact that one occurs earlier in the poem, if not earlier in "real" time.

The answer to what happens to the Jeweller is that much "happens" to him—but not much in the way of change. The poem narrates nothing like a step-by-step development in understanding nor a gradual conversion of the will, although it does record a series of different attitudes and moods, some of which are good, and some foolish and sinful. The Jeweller's comments upon awakening help us readers to see the wrongness of his possessive and willful desire, but he still lacks the proper perspective about his dream and his pearl. Moreover, the poem does not say that gradually or even finally the Jeweller once and for all attains caritas, a state in which he is resigned and consoled to his loss, loving his God and hoping to join him in his kingdom. The narrative frame, which includes the present tense of his grief in the opening stanzas as well as the present tense of his resignation in the closing stanzas, suggests rather that the Jeweller continues to suffer grief, confusion, and longing for his pearl. Such a qualified consolation fits very well with the poet's worldview, as it emerges from his other poems. The poet could have ended the poem differently, by merging the Jeweller's voice with his teacher's (as Boethius does in the *Consolation of Philosophy*) or by leaving him at the culmination of his heavenly vision (which is the way Dante concludes *Paradiso*). By bringing the Dreamer out of his dream, the poet must bring him back to earth and earthliness. For the Pearl poet, human beings are a pretty sorry lot: weak and foolish creatures, who, even when they know, when they have been told, and they have read, and they have seen the truth of Christianity, do not give up their mortal longings and misunderstandings. As long as they remain in this world, in this time, and in this space, they will be burdened by their mortality. And this is why the Jeweller does not achieve the complete enlightenment of revelatory vision and why the Jeweller—as dreamer, narrator, and poet—can both experience the dream and craft the poem, without fully realizing what he has heard and seen or without integrating his different perspectives and his different selves.

The Pearl

The one clear development in the poem and in the dream is in the change in what a pearl seems to be and to represent. This is not so much a matter of change as it is of accumulation; in other words, "pearl" gathers meanings and uses, so that by the end of the poem it refers to, represents, and is many things. Before tracing this movement and accumulation in the poem, we ought first to set the terms for our discussion, terms I think best taken from medieval thinking about language. Today we tend to use the terms "signifier" and "signified," and one of the strongest held views today is that the relationship between signifier and signified is arbitrary, and further that words, as well as other signs, carry meaning more in the context of other signs from which they differ than in and of themselves. Whether or not this view of language is correct (mostly it has been accepted, although not unqualifiedly), it is probably not the way most medieval readers or writers, the Pearl poet in particular, would have seen the situation.

More useful, though tricky, for discussing the Pearl poet's use of words is what Augustine says about language and signs. Using the terms *signum* (sign) and *res* (thing), Augustine distinguishes between a "res" that is only a "res" and a "res" that is also a "signum." He points out that there are some *signa* "whose whole purpose is in signifying, like words."[20] In the second book of *Christian Doctrine,* Augustine divides signs into two kinds, the "natural" and the "conventional" (2.1.2; p. 34), the latter classification sounding much like the "arbitrary" signs of modern sign theory, although it is important to recognize that "arbitrary" is a rather loaded term, which does not fit with a worldview of divinely sanctioned meaning and purpose throughout time and space. Furthermore, Augustine believed that meaning is the whole purpose of conventional signs. He states, "Nor is there any other reason for giving signs, except for bringing forth and transferring to another mind the action of the mind in the person who makes the sign" (1.2.3; p. 35). Using this terminology, we could take the word "pearl" as a signum, but since pearls are concrete objects, "pearl" is also a res that is used as a signum, one with conventional meaning, since its symbolism is not "natural" to it, as smoke is to fire, or footprints is to animal (the two examples Augustine uses for natural signs). The situation is complicated by the possibility that "pearl" (or "Margaret" or some variation, which comes from the French for "pearl") may be a person's name; even if the girl who died at a young age was not named "Pearl" or "Margaret," she carries that name, as a kind of title or epithet (similar to "queen" or "beautiful").[21]

The use of "Pearl" as a name is clearest in the poem's opening apostrophe to "Pearl" (the first word in the poem), lines that are very like those of a love lyric addressed to the poet's beloved lady, called here "Pearl." But "pearl" is not just a title or name, it is from the beginning a characteristic: the lady or girl is described figuratively as a pearl, one set in gold, round, and smooth. Furthermore, the poet speaks of himself as someone who deals in pearls (judging them, setting them), and shortly into the poem he is called a "jueler" (jeweller), both by himself (252) and by the Maiden (264) who has been identified as his pearl. Thus, already by the end of the first five sections, "pearl" is used several ways: as a name or title; as an actual pearl that falls to the ground; and as a metaphor that likens a person to the jewel, which in turn is extended to include a metaphor that likens the poet and his dreaming self to a jeweller.

In addition, the Maiden, whom the Dreamer calls "my pearl," is wearing pearls: actual, literal pearls (except, of course, that they appear in a dream within a poem, in which there is no such thing as actual, literal pearls). One of the pearls the Maiden wears stands out among the others that bedeck her clothing—the "wonder perle withouten wemme" (221; the marvelous spotless pearl)—which is set in the middle of her breast. The way in which this particular pearl is featured and the fact that it is where the Pearl Maiden's heart would be and that all the 144,000 wear such a pearl has led critics to associate it, quite sensibly, with the soul, or more precisely with the saved soul (Robertson 1950, 25–26).[22]

The Pearl Maiden later refers to the Parable of the Pearl of Great Price (Matt. 13:45–46), a very brief parable of a man (who significantly is labeled a "jueler"—729, 733), who sold all his goods to obtain a precious pearl. In the commonly held reading of this parable, the pearl represents salvation, and certainly that is one meaning for "pearl" in this poem. Actually what Jesus says in his parable is that the kingdom of heaven is like a merchant's search for fine pearls, which indicates that it is the story that provides an analogy, rather than the thing that works as a sign. Thus "pearl" is not just one saved soul, but the salvation promised to everyone—it is all the saved, the whole community of God's people celebrating his glory. The Jeweller, however, is all too inclined to think in terms of one pearl, his "priuy" (private, unique) pearl. Even by the end of the poem, when the Jeweller has seen the company of 144,000, all "pearls" wearing "pearls," when he can pray that God will make him one of the pearls, even then the Jeweller still marks out one special pearl, "my pearl," who is Pearl, as well as being a saved soul wearing pearls. While the Jeweller focuses on one pearl, the dream and the poem move to a consideration of pearls as a group, the blessed of heaven.

The images and terms used for the pearls who are the blessed tell us much about the qualities and meanings of pearl and also about the Jeweller's degree of understanding. Two of the Jeweller's terms for the company of pearls are especially revealing: the first, used when he recounts the vision, is "His meyny schene" (1145; His [God's] shining company); and the second, which comes in the final prayer, is "His homly hyne" (1211; His household servants). The term used in the poet's prayer is a humbler one, for although *homly* in Middle English is not as homely and inelegant as its modern equivalent, it does suggest a kind of ordinary domesticity, as does *hyne,* a word used for common laborers and servants. *Meyny,* on the other hand, is a little less lowly, for it is generally used for the followers or retinue of a lord, while *schene* elevates the company to the shining light of heaven. Characteristic of the Pearl poet (and indeed of much fourteenth-century poetry) is this combination of ordinariness and transcendence. A pearl too, as the concrete, literal gem, combines these characteristics, for, while it lacks the dazzling colors or lights of gems like rubies and emeralds, it is perfect in its roundness (circles and spheres being conventional figures for perfection and eternity) and in its spotlessness—a pearl is both *homly* and *schene.*

The Poem and the Modes of Parable, Vision, and Sacrament

The two views of pearls and of the company of pearls closely parallel the modes and styles of the poem's two main biblical sources. It is no accident that the poet has used two such different biblical passages: one a parable from Matthew's Gospel and the other a vision from John's Apocalypse. Both of these passages concern the subject of the kingdom of God, for the Parable of the Vineyard is about how God rewards his workers with entrance into his kingdom, while the vision of the New Jerusalem shows us what that kingdom is like. Yet the styles, the modes, and the genres of the two passages are very different. The Parable of the Vineyard is, as I have pointed out, not visual, but verbal, even more so in the Pearl Maiden's paraphrasing and exegesis than in the biblical text. Like the phrase "homly hyne," the parable is of the workaday world; it is a story of people busying themselves with their earthly affairs. Such is the nature of the genre, for parables are characteristically simple tales of everyday life, drawn from the world of the audience, tales that teach a lesson. (Although patristic exegesis had been inclined to allegorize parables quite elaborately, the genre originally is less allegorical than illustrative, and this is the way the Pearl poet uses it.[23])

The vision of the New Jerusalem and of the 144,000, which actually draws on several of John's visions in the Apocalypse, is as visual as the parable is verbal. The vision belongs to the same mode as the phrase "meyny schene," for it shines with a heavenly transcendence. And whereas, by teaching one principal point the parable works like an *exemplum* (a short, illustrative story, much used in medieval sermons), the visions are rich in multiple symbols and meanings: the New Jerusalem, the Wedding of the Lamb, and the Lamb with his company—-the 144,000, the elders, and the angels around the Throne—all singing the new song.

We should note that the implicit dichotomy between the verbal, dialectic mode of the parable and the visual, symbolic mode of the visions is a limitation, owing in part to their respective relationships to historical reality, and indicative of their incompleteness as signs. Neither is an actual event: one is an exemplary story that is not literally true, but true because it illustrates truth; and the other is a revelatory dream, which though divinely sent does not record past or present reality, but rather is a picture of the future, of things to come. There are, in fact, only oblique references in *Pearl* to any actual events of salvation history—when the Pearl Maiden distinguishes between the New Jerusalem and the old one, and when the Dreamer sees (and notably misunderstands) the Lamb's wound. In this respect, *Pearl* is quite different from *Cleanness* and *Patience,* both of which retell actual biblical events, although each of these latter poems reveals a similar dichotomy between visual and verbal modes in the Bible.

Finally, the poem itself, entitled "Pearl" by modern editors (there is no title given in the one surviving manuscript), is both a dazzling jewel, with brilliant craftmanship, and an earthbound record of a dream. As we have seen, the poem, for the most part, avoids the experience of transcendence; the vision of the New Jerusalem is secondhand, and even that secondhand view is interrupted. On the other hand, while lacking the immediacy of direct experience, the vision that climaxes the poem includes bright and vivid images that capture the brilliance of the richly illuminated manuscripts of John's Apocalypse. The same combination of earthliness with transcendence can be found in the dream's discourse, which includes both sophisticated language games and lively, realistic dialogue, and is also exemplified in the nearly perfect artistry of its versification.

There is no single, lasting resolution to these two levels and styles, any more than there is one resolved meaning for "pearl" or a clear permanent progress for the Jeweller. However, the poem's final stanza does indicate one partial resolution to the tension and contrast between earthly and heavenly and between artfully elegant and down-to-earth. Although the poem and the dream and the poet are all finally earthbound and cannot remain in heaven or in any vision or poem of heaven, they can be transformed into a different mode from the usual one of earthly time and space: the mode of prayer and sacrament, which is invoked in the poem's final stanza.

In this final stanza the Jeweller effects a transformation of his poem and his experience by offering them, along with his pearl, to God:

> Ouer þis hyul þis lote I laȝte,
> For pyty of my perle enclyin,
> And syþen to God I hit bytaȝte,
> In Krystez dere blessyng and myn,
> Þat in þe forme of bred and wyn
> Þe preste vus schewez vch a daye.
>
> Over this hillock I received this *lote,*
> As I lay mourning my pearl,
> And then I committed "it" to God,
> With Christ's dear blessing and mine,
> That in the form of bread and wine
> The priest shows to us every day.
>
> (1205–10)

This is a difficult stanza to read and harder to translate, partly because it relies on ambiguity both of vocabulary (especially the word *lote*) and of syntax and grammar. The Middle English word *lote* has the same root as our word *lots* (as in "casting lots") and means here "chance" or "chance event." In addition, there almost certainly is a pun on another Middle English word *lote,* which means "speech" or "word" (Andrew and Waldron, eds., 110, note to lines 1205–10). Thus, what the Jeweller receives while mourning his pearl is both the experience of the dream, including the words of the Pearl Maiden, and also the words that are the poem he writes about the dream. Moreover, the lines in which the Jeweller commends the pearl to God contain an ambiguous pronoun, "hit," which could refer both to "my perle," which is the nearest antecedent, and I think also to "lote," since that is the nearest antecedent not in a parenthetical remark.[24]

The closing lines thus suggest that the Jeweller has received the experience of the dream and the words or teaching of his pearl and that he is returning that pearl and that "lote," the experience and the words of the poem, to God. This process of receiving and then offering in return involves a transformation very like the one that takes place in the Mass, and it is therefore no coincidence that it is described in a stanza that both refers to the Mass and ends with a prayer. The sacramental mode of the poem's last stanza thus involves the poem itself, as well as the Jeweller and his pearl. In eucharistic theology, the bread and wine that the congregation offers as gifts to God are transformed into Christ's body and blood (which the people see when the priest elevates them), and then are given back to the faithful Christians in the Eucharist, when they receive the body and blood of Christ. So too the poem begins with the Jeweller's grief for his pearl, which results in the dream that is sent to him, which he records in his poem, all of which he commends to God, with the hope and prayer that he too can become part of God's kingdom, one of the "homly hyne." Only the sacramental mode of the last stanza can bring the Jeweller to this contented hopefulness, in which he is resigned to his loss, because here he offers the pearl and his dream to God. In this offering, his poem is transformed, so that, while still the product of the earthbound Jeweller, the poem can also incorporate the enlightened views of the Pearl Maiden and her teaching, as well as the transcendent vision of the New Jerusalem. When transformed, the lowly "homly hyne" are indeed the same as the glorious "meyny schene."

The Jeweller, a role that includes the poet, as well as the fallible and foolish Dreamer, is both inside and outside the dream; he is at once the grief-stricken narrator of the opening lines, the remorseful, eventually resigned, narrator of the closing stanzas, and the poet who crafts the poem. Because the change takes place in the sacramental mode, not in historical time, it is not a finished event, but rather coexists alongside the poem's account of past experiences (the dream sent to the Dreamer) and its present grief and mourning. Unlike Boethius in the *Consolation of Philosophy,* or Dante in the *Divine Comedy,* the Jeweller in *Pearl* cannot maintain his enlightened state, for it does not even fully exist within the poem, but only partially within the sacramental mode invoked in the last stanza.

If we have read the poem carefully and, as much as possible, experienced the dream with the Dreamer, we should by the end be ready to give up our earthbound need to have a single definition for "pearl," to "sette hyr sengely in synglure" (8; set her uniquely in uniqueness), as the Jeweller longs to do. We should also cease looking for one sensible answer as to whether the Dreamer is consoled or enlightened. Maintaining the sense of both a fallible, grief-stricken dreamer, who only partially understands the Pearl Maiden's message, along with a clear-eyed poet, who releases his hold on the pearl and his grief for her, demands the kind of balancing act required to hold the accumulation of many meanings for "pearl." As readers, we need to see that complete answers are no more possible than full enlightenment.

This poem, the most transcendent of the Pearl poet's works, is a testimony to how earthbound this poet is. Even in a dream poem, with brilliantly crafted versification and highly conventional motifs, he bumps back to earth frequently, worrying about such things as how a pack of jewels will manage if they have to "camp out." Even when writing about apocalyptic vision, the Pearl poet does not ascend to any kind of direct mystical experience, nor can he find his own words to describe heaven, but rather he must keep grounding himself in his biblical text. Always he comes back to the "homly." In fact, he is a poet much more comfortable with actual, historical events than with dreams or visions, and his Christianity is not one of theological speculation or mystical experiences, but rather is firmly rooted in the Bible and in the history it records. In the next two poems in the manuscript, *Cleanness* and *Patience,* the Pearl poet turns to biblical history and to narrative, and away from the vision and the dream world and the sophisticated verse and language of *Pearl.*

Chapter Three
Cleanness

Cleanness, the second longest of the four poems in the Cotton Nero manuscript, is a biblical narrative, actually a series of narratives, all but one taken from the Book of Genesis: two brief accounts of the falls from grace that begin providential history; the story of Noah and the Flood; the story of Sodom and Gomorrah; and an account from the Book of Daniel of Belshazzar's Feast, which contains the Writing on the Wall episode. The poem also includes a retelling of the Parable of the Wedding Feast from Matthew's Gospel, which serves as an introduction to the Old Testament narratives.

Frequently referred to as "Purity" (one, but only one, of the possible translations of the Middle English word *cleanness*) and described as a "verse homily" by most critics, this is the least read and least liked of the Pearl poet's poems. There are several good, or at least seemingly valid, reasons for its unpopularity. Even without its title or genre label—both of them misleading and both assigned by nineteenth- and twentieth-century scholars—*Cleanness* in itself is a forbidding and uncongenial poem. It depicts an angry and vengeful God who repeatedly destroys his creation and his creatures, and a series of rather wimpish and certainly uninteresting protagonists, not one of whom engages our attention, much less our sympathies. Clearly, *Cleanness* does not appeal to modern taste—in fact, and this is important to keep in mind, the poem probably did not appeal much to medieval taste either. Furthermore, the several narratives in *Cleanness,* aside from their linkage through chronological arrangement, have seemed to most readers to be disconnected tales, joined only by their common theme of "uncleanness", whatever that may be, and by their common type as "negative exempla": illustrative stories that demonstrate a way *not* to behave. It is partly because the rhetorical strategy of using illustrative stories about one topic characterizes many medieval sermons that critics have called *Cleanness* a "verse homily."

But, while unpopular and somewhat distasteful, *Cleanness* is neither a bad poem nor even a boring one, and it is certainly not a dull sermon set in rhyme. *Cleanness* does, however, require a certain adjustment of our views and some preparation to be appreciated. We need to know what it is really about, which is not just sexual purity, but rather the nearly hopeless relationship between a terrifying, angry Creator and his repulsively wicked creatures. The Pearl poet is at pains in *Cleanness* to make us see how terrible, though true, this view is, especially in light of the shining, spotless beauty of God's kingdom, the same transcendent and unearthly beauty featured in the vision of *Pearl*. This beauty, *Cleanness* tells us, is what humanity is made for and this is what they so disgustingly and completely do not deserve.

The reading of *Cleanness* as a "verse homily" and a compilation of several instances of a narrative type labeled "negative exempla" suffers from two misleading critical approaches. First, it is based on the modern preference for "organic unity," a preference that has recently been strongly questioned and revised by literary theorists, who have shown that critics have more often than not imposed this aesthetic ideal on texts by skillfully ignoring all of a text's inherent contradictions and disunities. Today, even though most of us still expect some kind of unity in a text, we are inclined to accept variety and digressions more than we used to, and most of us have learned not to look down on episodic narratives as necessarily clumsy or weak.[1] Thus, the fact that *Cleanness* tells not one story but several, and that it has not one single protagonist but several,[2] is, according to recent critical taste, not such a bad thing.

As for the view that *Cleanness* is a "verse homily," this works like so many half-truths about literature, closing off readers' minds rather than opening them. The term "verse homily" serves to reduce this poem to the status of a didactic sermon, one that tediously piles on several instances of human impurity and divine wrath. However, although *Cleanness* is certainly a poem with a strong moral lesson, and one that definitely speaks of the *contraré* of *clannes,* as well as of God's anger, it is much longer and more complex than a sermon could be, and its narratives, except for the first two, which do not really concern "clannes," are also too long and too involved to qualify as the usual exempla employed in sermons. Furthermore, the tales in *Cleanness* are not just repetitions, but variations, and they are not just strung along in a series, but rather are set in a framing narrative. That framing narrative traces several themes, as noted by the poem's best critics: the definition of "clannes" itself; the "pattern of judgment";[3] "the realities of justice and mercy in terms of human choice," particularly in terms of "the three classic sins of lust, avarice, and pride";[4] and "the re-creation of concrete meanings for moral *clannes* and moral *fylthe*" (Spearing 1970, 52).

In addition to these unifying themes, I would add the poem's development of an overall narrative, the story of God's anger at his creatures. To tell this story in *Cleanness,* the poet has selected a few important episodes from his audience's earliest and most sacred history. According to *Cleanness,* this history records not just humanity's repeated and increasing sinfulness, but also God's increasing withdrawal from the ugliness of that sinfulness and the world in which it thrives. The first stories tell of a God who is close to his creation and his creatures, who speaks directly to them, who reacts like an impatient but loving father, expressing strong feelings and regrets about his children's bad behavior. But God's disgust with his creation apparently causes him to withdraw, so that by the third major narrative of the poem God no longer speaks to human beings or sends them messengers to speak in his name. Instead, he remains distant from his corrupted creation and communicates with mankind through obscure written messages that require an interpreter. The Pearl poet records this tale of God's increasing anger and consequent absence through a favorite tactic (which he uses also in the famous hunting and bedroom scenes in *Gawain*): the use of parallel episodes that call attention to their similarities and differences. Although the narrator rarely makes explicit comparisons between these episodes, he does offer clues, in the Prologue especially, that help readers to follow the poem's various thematic developments and its framing narrative. To demonstrate how this is accomplished, I will turn now to a detailed discussion of the Prologue, and then move on to a consideration of the poem's main narratives, taking them up in the order in which they appear in the poem.

The Prologue of *Cleanness*

Cleanness begins with a prologue in which the narrator announces his topic, in what would be a standard rhetorical opening, except for one critical detail: the thematic focus of the poem is not the one explicitly named in the first word of the first line, but rather the one implicitly alluded to in a prepositional phrase in the fourth line. What the narrator actually says is:

> Clannesse whoso kyndly cowþe comende,
> And rekken vp alle þe resounz þat ho by riȝt askeȝ,
> Fayre formez myȝt he fynde in forering his speche,
> And in þe contraré kark and combraunce huge.

> Cleanness—whoever could praise it appropriately
> And reckon up all the evidence that she rightfully demands,
> Fair forms would he find in fashioning his speech,
> And in the contrary trouble and a huge burden.
>
> $$(1-4)^5$$

Thus, in praising "clannes" one would have much material and "fayre formez" at hand. "Fayre formez" is often translated as "beautiful or noble themes," but I believe it is a much more inclusive phrase, referring not just to themes and topics, but also to rhetorical and poetic figures, and even stories (cf. Vantuono, ed.).

To do the "contraré" [the opposite] of praising "clannes" is a burdensome task, with the implication that the contraré is exactly what the poet is going to do. However, it is important to note that the poet's project is only implied; indeed not all readers infer that the poet will be attempting the "contrary" of praising cleanness. Moreover, what exactly constitutes the "contrary" is not itself explicit; some readers have thought the contrary of praising cleanness ought to be condemning it, others thought that the contrary would be praising *uncleanness,* and a few that the contrary must be condemning uncleanness.[6] Certainly, the syntax of these opening lines is loose and therefore their meaning is somewhat ambiguous, but I believe the poet is speaking of the mirror opposites of both verb and object: "condemn" instead of "praise," and "uncleanness" instead of "cleanness."

This is, in fact, the way the entire poem works: it praises cleanness by condemning uncleanness, it celebrates salvation through Christ by recounting instances of divine condemnation, and it affirms God's presence for the good Christian by depicting his absence from the wicked. The poet rarely refers to the beauty of cleanness, or to Christian salvation, or to the divine presence, except in a few places, and significantly these references lie outside the recounted events of sacred history. Even less explicit than the celebration of cleanness is its definition. The poet makes us work hard to understand what *clannes* is: through illustrative events we are meant to infer first what uncleanness is, and then from that already secondhand inference, we must conclude thirdhand just exactly what constitutes cleanness. In addition, for its subject term, *clannes,* the poem *Cleanness* does what *Pearl* does for its topic of the pearl: accumulating meanings, some of them fairly farfetched, rather than restricting or clarifying them. *Cleanness* begins with the obvious literal and figural uses of cleanness—as clean garments and pure virtue—and then stretches both literal and figural as far as possible, indeed beyond possible to paradox and oxymoron.

The major portion of the Prologue is taken up with a retelling of the Parable of the Wedding Feast—taken, as the narrator tells us, from the Gospel of Matthew (22:1–14). This parable tells of a king who invites guests to a wedding banquet for his son. When all repeatedly refuse to attend and some even murder the servants who bring them the invitation, the king extends his invitation to anyone who wants to come, but then punishes one last-minute guest who arrives without a proper wedding garment. At first reading, Matthew's Parable of the Wedding Feast would seem consistent with the Pearl poet's themes of uncleanness and divine punishment. It is noteworthy too that Matthew's version does this better than the similar parable told in Luke's gospel (14:16–24). Luke's comparable parable is a pleasanter story; it lacks the violence of Matthew's: no murder of the king's servants, no unworthily dressed guest bound and thrown out into the darkness. The differences between Luke's and Matthew's versions of this parable are important to understanding *Cleanness,* for it is precisely the unpleasant "extras" in Matthew's version that constitute the "kark and combaunce huge" (4; trouble and huge burden) of writing about the "contraré" of "clanness." Matthew's parable shows an angry and vengeful lord, much closer than Luke's is to the punishing god who destroys evildoers with flood and fire. In addition to choosing Matthew's version as his source, the poet emphasizes its darker side by telling his own little parable beforehand, a story about a feast and a poorly dressed guest in a contemporaneous context; there is no mention in this "mini-parable" of the repeated invitations to the banquet, much less of the inclusion of those normally excluded.

On the other hand, although offering a more troubling story than Luke's, Matthew's parable is basically of the same kind. Both of these parables have been classified by modern biblical scholarship as "parables of the kingdom"—so-called because they describe the kingdom of God. Their most important "givens" are that such a kingdom exists, that it is less earthly than the one the victorious Israelite nation had looked for in the past, and that it is available to all. In certain of the parables of the kingdom, Jesus emphasizes the extension of divine salvation, away from the Jews, who are often portrayed as rejecting his message, to all the world. This is the heart of both Luke's and Matthew's parables of the feast, and this lesson, repressed in the poet's mini-parable and less clear in his retelling of Matthew's version, is emphasized in the brief aphorism that concludes Matthew's parable: "Many are called but few are chosen." Oddly, and seemingly inconsistently, the Pearl poet not only retains this saying at the end of his paraphrase of Matthew's parable, he makes it even more hopeful and less threatening by dropping the negative second half, saying only: "Thus comparisunez Kryst þe kyndom of heuen / To þis frelych feste þat fele arn to called" (161–62; Thus has Christ compared the kingdom of heaven to this glorious feast to which many are called).

Like the entire poem, the Prologue emphasizes God's punishing anger, while also reminding us of his open invitation to the eternal feast. The figure of the heavenly banquet, while only occasionally used in the Gospels, would have been a rich and evocative one for the poem's audience, since it was a popular image in exegesis and iconography. The image accords well with the role of the Eucharist in a Christian's life, and also with the motif of the Wedding of the Lamb. In the Latin Bible, the word used in Luke's parable is *cena* (supper), the same word used for the Last Supper and the Eucharist in Latin Christianity. The word in Matthew's parable, *nuptiae* (wedding), connects the story to the Wedding of the Lamb, an eschatological image suggested by a few brief references in the Book of Revelation (see especially 19:7, 21:2) and much developed by later Christian tradition. By using the English word for Luke's term (Middle English *feste* for Latin *cena*), while retelling Matthew's version with the wedding, the Pearl poet is able to connect both images—feast and wedding celebration—to the banquet awaiting Christians at the end of time.

In his comments that link the parable to the series of Old Testament narratives that form the main body of the poem, the narrator further links the heavenly feast to the beatific vision, the promise that the saved will see God "face to face" (as Paul puts it in 1 Corinthians 13:12). In *Cleanness* the narrator promises that all those who are "fetyse of a fayr forme" (174; adorned with a lovely form) and covered "ful clene" (175; with complete cleanliness; competely) will "se þy Sauior and His sete ryche" (176; see thy Savior and his glorious throne).

Although later in the poem the narrator reminds readers of the promise of the beatific vision and the joys of heaven, the dark threat of rejection from those joys predominates over the promise itself, both in the individual narratives and in the framing story that connects them. One important exception to this theme of unrelenting and even increasing anger—the passage on the Incarnation that comes between the story of Sodom and Gomorrah and the story of Belshazzar's Feast—is also an exception to the chronology of the framing narrative. Because it stands as an intrusion, I would like to leave the Incarnation passage for later and turn first to each of the Old Testament narratives that make up the main body of the poem.

Cleanness's Story of God's Anger

The two falls, the Fall of the Angels and the Fall of Adam, begin the main narrative of *Cleanness,* as they began providential history. Both falls are recounted in spare, almost paradigmatic form. The Fall of Lucifer and his "fenden folk" (224; fiendish folk) occupies but 30 lines, and the brevity of its telling parallels the swiftness with which God executes the punishment. Lucifer's unnatural and traitorous return for the fair beauty God has bestowed on him is to claim equality with God in a two-line boast:

> "I schal telde vp my trone in þe tramountayne,
> And by lyke to þat Lorde þat þe lyft made."

> "I shall raise up my throne in the north
> And become like the Lord that made the heavens."
>
> (211–12)

God's judgment comes instantly with this boast: "With þis worde þat he warp, þe wrake on him lyȝt" (213; With this word that he spoke, the vengeance fell on him). The "feloun" (evildoer), who prided himself so on his "fayre wedez" (217; beautiful garments), turns instantly to black hideousness as he falls from heaven.

The story of the Fall of Adam, even briefer than the story of the Fall of the Angels, takes up a mere 13 lines. As in the story of Lucifer, God does not speak but simply condemns, acting swiftly and silently. However, unlike the Fall of the Angels, which is never reversed (since, as we are told, the fiend is too proud to make peace), the Fall of Adam is to be emended through "a mayden þat make had neuer" (248; a maid who never had an equal or a mate).[7] The punishment of Adam is therefore less final than Lucifer's and significantly less ugly, for it contains nothing comparable to the descriptive details given of the falling black fiends, who are like a swarming hive or dark smoke. Instead, the Fall of Adam closes with a reminder of the promise of the Incarnation.

From these two brief stories that begin history, the poem moves to the first of its major narratives, the Flood. In contrast to the Fall of Adam, the story of the Flood is told at length, in an expanded, but also a streamlined, paraphrase of the Genesis account. The story begins with God's anger over the "fylþe vpon folde þat þe folk vsed" (251; the filth that people practiced on earth) and his regret that he has made his creation (285). Vowing to destroy his creation, God then speaks to Noah of his plan to flood the earth and commands him to build the ark.

To the Genesis account the poet adds a few descriptive details about the coming of the Flood and even more about the victims and their suffering. Here he draws on his great skill in "pointing" and provides a vivid picture of the catastrophic event. Alliterative verse in the hands of a master, here as elsewhere, proves marvelously effective for doing the "big scene" (such as storms, wars, or feasts). In addition to expanding the biblical account in certain places, the poet also prunes some details, specifically those that are awkward inconsistencies and those that do not fit with the main development of the poem's overall story. For example, repetitious and inconsistent details about the number of animals taken into the ark (see Genesis 6:20 and 7:2), which worried even the earliest exegetes, are, in *Cleanness,* simply conflated and resolved into one command to Noah to take at least a pair of every kind of living creature, and of the clean ones seven pairs (334).

One remarkable omission in the Pearl poet's recounting of the Flood is the lack of any reference to the rainbow, which in Genesis God says is the "sign of the covenant" between him and all living creatures, a promise that he will never again send a flood to destroy the whole earth (9:11–17). The rainbow has understandably been a favorite sign of God's love for both Jews and Christians. I think the poet's omission of this sign was intentional and is revealing of his concerns. It offers evidence of the underlying frame narrative of *Cleanness,* the historical development of God's way of communicating with his creatures, from the direct, spoken word, which is clear and present, to the increasingly indirect means sent from a distant deity. This development, this falling-off from a close "I–Thou" relationship to a distant one, is a move from presence to absence. At the time of the Flood, God is still present and close. When he promises never again to send a flood or to destroy all of his creation, he speaks to Noah "in comly comfort ful clos and cortays wordez" (512; in gracious comfort with intimate, courteous words); there is no need for a visual symbol or any kind of mediating sign when God is so near and his voice can be heard.

Throughout the story of the Flood, the conversations between God and Noah have been simple and direct—even when they are not comforting, as they certainly are not when God first speaks to Noah of his anger and his planned vengeance, even then the message is clear and God's voice is present and real. Similarly, Noah confines his speech to simple answers to God; he does not question, he does not argue, and we never see him grumbling as he does in the popular mystery plays—all is readiness and obedience, epitomized in the first words we hear Noah speak: "Ʒe Lorde, with Þy leue" (347; Yes, Lord, with Thy leave). Noah does not act on his own—he does not even steer the ark, which in fact has no rudder or sail or any other means of maneuvering, but is in the complete control of God, who is the "lodezmon" (424; pilot). The simple directness of the conversations between God and Noah and the complete dependence of Noah upon God are mirrored in the plot of the Flood story, which moves straightforwardly from God's regret over his creation and his projected vengeance, to the climactic execution of that vengeance, and the denouement of God's promise to send no more floods, a promise that implies a new regret, this time about his destruction instead of his creation.

The implication that God can change his mind, suggested by his expressions of regret over sending a destructive flood, becomes stronger in the remaining stories in *Cleanness*. In the accounts of Sodom and Gomorrah and Belshazzar's Feast, God's judgment is less direct, less final, and the divine presence less felt; now providential history is moving from presence to absence, from spoken reality to unspoken signs. The plots of both these narratives move forward less directly, with God even hesitating over his actions, and there are subplots and imbedded stories that suggest alternative endings.

In neither the Sodom and Gomorrah story nor its subnarrative of Abraham's Visitors is there anything as reassuring as the loving God who speaks to Noah in "comly comfort" (512; gracious comfort) and takes full command of the ark; nor is there anything so horrifying as the wrath of the Creator who regrets his own creation. In the Sodom and Gomorrah section there is also more possibility for equivocation, for arguing with God's Word, or for disobeying him. Humanity and their words take on greater force and become increasingly important, attaining in Sodom and Gomorrah a certain real power in salvation history, albeit as often for evil as for good. God is further away and his role is reduced. Once humanity has an opportunity to speak to God with more than Noah's simple answers of assent and once God's creatures begin to participate in their own salvation, the question of delaying or mitigating God's judgment arises, so that the more complex relationship of God with his people leads to a more complicated narrative. In the story of Abraham's Visitors, the announcement to Abraham of the fate of the two cities does not have the finality of God's first speech to Noah, since it quickly turns into a bargaining session, in which Abraham keeps asking God to spare the cities if he can find just 50 good people, or even 40, and so on, until God is talked down to as few as 10 righteous creatures, for the sake of whom he will cancel his planned destruction of the cities.

Furthermore, unlike the pure voice in the Flood story, which is simply identified as God, the Three Visitors who appear to Abraham are not God, but an appearance of him. Although visualized, Abraham's Visitors are paradoxically less present and less real than the unseen voice of the Lord in the Flood story. In this respect they are more messengers from God than God himself. In *Cleanness* the Visitors evoke God, but they behave like any honored guests: talking to Abraham, sharing a meal with him, and explaining God's plan. The Pearl poet casts this episode in a well-realized scene, with the trappings of human civilization; to what he already had to work with in Genesis he adds more details to give us a pleasant picture of a kind of medieval picnic. All of this is markedly different from the conversations between God and Noah, which seem to exist in no earthly space. It is as though the divine has been domesticated in the scene with Abraham. But what this scene gains in familiarity, it loses in transcendence.

The main narrative in the Sodom and Gomorrah story, the actual condemnation of the cities and the saving of Lot, further develops the possibilities for modifying God's Word that are found in Abraham's bargaining session. Lot is allowed to converse freely with the bearers of God's Word. When he does not understand how he will escape God's wrath, he questions the angels in anguish:

> Þen laled Loth: "Lorde, what is best?
> If I me fele vpon fote þat I fle moȝt,
> Hov schulde I huyde me fro Hym þat hatz His hate kynned
> In þe brath of His breth þat brennez all þinkez?"

> Then Lot said: "Lord, what is best?
> If I go out on foot so that I can flee,
> How can I hide from Him who has inflamed his anger
> In the fury of his breath that can burn up all things.

(913–16)

Lot is all too aware of the power of God's wrath, but he is assured that he will be allowed to flee, and he is given the right to name his own place of refuge. Lot's speech is freer than Abraham's—less formal, less couched in humble, apologetic civilities. Furthermore, Lot's role in saving his family is greater than Abraham's or Noah's. Lot is left to rouse his family, to choose his destination, and even to defend, or attempt to defend, his sacred visitors when they fall under the threat of the Sodomites' sexual desires. In this story God's people do not merely say "Yes" with ready obedience as Noah does; instead they discuss the details of the providential plan, a plan that begins to be contingent, not final.

Some of God's creatures do more than argue politely, like Abraham and Lot. Sarah, Lot's wife, and the Sodomites at Lot's door challenge and even scorn God's judgment. Sarah laughs at God's promise of a son (655–56); and Lot's wife not only scoffs at the command to use no salt in her cakes (822–24) but flatly disobeys the prohibition, resulting in defilement of the holy angels. The ultimate scorn of God and the most obscene defilement of his angels come with the "harlotez speche" (874; whores' speech) of the Sodomites at Lot's door, as they demand to practice their filthy sin on God's representatives.

In contrast to the concentrated drama in the Flood, the climax of the story of Sodom and Gomorrah moves back and forth, from the storm of fire and brimstone, to the flight of Lot and his family, to Abraham, and then back to the end of the fire with a description of the Dead Sea, which is all that remains of the destroyed cities of the plain. The sulphurous stench of the Dead Sea, the unnaturalness of this dead water and the vegetation that surround it, mark the close of the second main narrative—in strong contrast to the promise God speaks to Noah after the Flood. In place of God's own words that end the Flood story, the Sodom and Gomorrah story ends with the poet's comments on the story's moral, a warning to his audience to "clene worþe" (1056; become clean) if they want to enjoy the beatific vision. God is not present at the end of this story—instead we have only the hope that someday we might "se þat Semly in sete and His swete face" (1055; see that Fair One on His throne and [look upon] His sweet face).

Belshazzar's Feast, the last of the "þrynne wyses" (1805; three ways) that the poet tells to demonstrate how God is driven away by filth, is the most complicated narrative in the poem. Its plot is less spare and less focused than those of the earlier stories, and the narrative line less clear, as is the relationship between God and his people. In this narrative God does not appear to Belshazzar, nor does he speak directly to him, nor does he even send his messengers, as he does to Abraham and Lot. He communicates only through secret written signs, which require human interpretation. God's punishments are likewise less direct; no longer "acts of God," they now work through human agents, the scourges of God.

At the center of the story of Belshazzar's Feast is the evil Babylonian king, Belshazzar, who is contrasted to his noble father Nebuchadnezzar (actually his grandfather in most of the biblical sources), whose conquest of Jerusalem and removal of the holy vessels from the temple provide the introduction to the main episode. Unlike his father, Belshazzar does not honor "Israel Dryȝten" (1314; the Israelites' God). He leads instead a life of sin and godlessness, which is climaxed by a great feast attended by nobles from all over his kingdom and by his concubines and wife. In his mad drunkenness at this feast, Belshazzar calls for the holy vessels from Jerusalem, drinks from one of the sacred cups, and passes them around to his concubines and knights to do the same. God then sends them a warning (1504), a "ferly" (1529; wonderous event), the famous Writing on the Wall.

None of the mighty king's wise men can understand this message, until, at the Queen's suggestion, the Israelite prophet Daniel is called. Daniel begins by telling the story of Nebuchadnezzar's own fault, the sin of pride, and the penance he served as a beast in the wilderness until God restored him to his reason and his throne. Then, after pointing out how different Belshazzar is from his father, Daniel reads and interprets the words on the wall: *Mane. Techal. Phares*—God has numbered your kingdom and marked its end; he has weighed your reign and found it wanting; your kingdom will be given to the Persians, and the Medes will be rulers here (1727–40; see Dan. 5:25–28). The feast ends quickly, and so does the story and the poem, with a silent invasion in the night by Darius and the Medes. The boastful, blasphemous king dies unheroically, beaten to death and left like a dog "þat in a dych lygges" (1792; that lies in a ditch). Unlike the earlier stories, there is no mention in Belshazzar's Feast of any surviving righteous remnant (even though there was, for the Book of Daniel tells us more about Daniel's life under the Medes and Persians, while the Book of Ezra, which continues the history of II Chronicles, narrates the restoration of the temple in Jerusalem).

The number of different sources for Belshazzar's Feast are an indication of the complexity of this story. Actually several conflated sources, these biblical texts do not form one single coherent passage, like the Genesis sources for the Flood and Sodom and Gomorrah. While the principal source for Belshazzar's Feast is chapter 5 of the Book of Daniel, the Pearl poet has also drawn on early chapters of Daniel, which describe the fall of Jerusalem to the Babylonians and the subsequent reign of Nebuchadnezzar. In addition, the poet has probably relied upon other books of the Old Testament for details or background to some of these events. For example, Exodus provides a description of the holy vessels that Belshazzar desecrates (compare especially Exodus 25:31–37 and *Cleanness* 1479–87), while the removal of the vessels to Babylon is recounted in II Chronicles (36:11–23), a passage that also includes surrounding events of the Babylonian exile, though not Belshazzar's Feast itself. The fall of Jerusalem and the end of the kingdom of Judah, recounted in II Chronicles, chapter 36, is narrated at greater length in Jeremiah (52:1–26).

Clearly, this part of providential history is different from the earliest events in the story of God and his creatures, for which the Book of Genesis is the sole source. Like the remnant of God's people scattered among many lands, the accounts of postexilic Israel are spread through several books, which overlap each other in chronology and are of different genres, some chronicled history, some prophetic books (which in turn can include poetry, commentary, historical accounts, and visions and their interpretation). For both Jews and Christians, these later events of providential history lack the authority and the holiness accorded to those of earliest times, which are recorded in Genesis and Exodus. I think it safe to assume that the Pearl poet not only recognized this lack of authority, but was well aware of the narrative complexity (more so for him than for us since it is very unlikely that he had at hand a Bible of his own through which to browse, much less one with cross-references). Moreover, I believe the poet found the lessened authority and increased complexity mirrored in the greater distance of God from his people— indeed, that distance is both cause and effect of the events themselves.

For all the disparate strands of his source materials and his narrative, the Pearl poet has skillfully formed them into one story, with an introduction, a careful buildup to the climactic scene, and a tidy, though grim, denouement. The story of Belshazzar's Feast is a well-told tale, more interesting and more exciting than the stories of Noah's Flood and Sodom and Gomorrah. It is also literally more dramatic and more theatrical: it has more "scenes," more characters, and a central villain, whose terrible deeds are actually described (in contrast to the earlier stories, especially the Flood, which mostly rely on indirect references rather than on direct accounts of the sins that provoke God's wrath).

One of the most telling differences between the story of Belshazzar's Feast and the two earlier major stories is the different role accorded to its hero Daniel, who is in many ways quite different from the patriarchs Noah, Abraham, and Lot, who lead their people and star in their stories (even if they star as unquestioning instruments for God's plan). Daniel is not a major player in biblical history, but rather a commentator, a preacher/teacher, who observes—in this case, literally reads—and interprets the events around him. Furthermore, unlike the earlier prophets, Amos and Jeremiah, for example, Daniel does not seem to hear the voice of God, much less to speak in God's voice—-rather, he must read the written message sent by God. (In fact, the Pearl poet has changed some of the details of Daniel's biblical story, in which he interprets dreams, both his own and others', in order to show him only interpreting the spoken or written words of God.)

Daniel's role is that of an apocalyptic seer, like John, the author of the immensely popular Book of the Revelation (known to the Middle Ages by its other title, the Apocalypse). The Book of Daniel, in fact, was included in many of the numerous lavishly illustrated manuscripts of the Apocalypse and its commentaries, in which an especially favorite scene for illustration was the Writing on the Wall—for medieval exegetes a preeminently apocalyptic event.

In addition to focusing on Daniel's role as visionary and seer, *Cleanness* in other respects is an apocalyptic poem. Like most apocalyptic texts, *Cleanness* is concerned with sin followed by cosmic punishment. All three of the major narratives retold in the poem are commonly held to be types of the End, events from Old Testament history that preshadow the events of the Last Days. While clearly eschatological, the earlier narratives of *Cleanness* lack some of the distinctive features scholars associate with apocalyptic texts, particularly the emphasis upon written and secret messages, and the resultant need for a seer to interpret. In this respect, Belshazzar's Feast is the most apocalyptic of the poem's three major stories, since its message is sent in mysterious signs, signs that no ordinary reader can interpret.

Furthermore, the story of Belshazzar's Feast exemplifies the parodoxes and contradictions inherent in the apocalyptic mode. For, while an apocalypse is by definition a "revelation," apocalyptic texts unfold their mysteries only through complex interpretation, and they frequently are at pains to disguise these revelations in arcane symbolism and strange visions. Although the revelation of divine purpose and of God himself is presumably the goal of apocalyptic vision, theophany is rare in most apocalypses and the words of God less present and less real than they are in either the Pentateuch or the prophets. Certainly, in *Cleanness* the absence of God is especially noticeable in Belshazzar's Feast, since it comes after the preceding stories in which God is more present—when Noah hears his voice, and Abraham and Lot are visited by messengers who speak for God (or are God).

In every respect, Belshazzar's Feast differs in degree and kind from the other narratives in *Cleanness*. In some respects, the time and place of this story seem much closer to that of the Pearl poet's fourteenth-century audience. However, while alike in their worldliness, in their distance from God and his voice, and in their loss of the geographical home for God's people, the audience of *Cleanness* and the world of post-exilic Babylon differ in one absolute and critical way: the people of Babylon—sinful idolators and righteous Jews alike—lack the truth of Christianity, and, more important, they lack the resources of the church and its sacraments. A critical moment in providential history—the Incarnation—separates the audience of *Cleanness* from the people in all of its stories. While this climactic moment of history is not narrated in *Cleanness,* it is the focus of the long interpolated passage that separates the last two narratives, Sodom and Gomorrah and Belshazzar's Feast. A close examination of the Incarnation passage will reveal some startling challenges and contradictions to the poem's underlying assumptions and explicit themes. I would like, then, to conclude this chapter on *Cleanness* with a discussion of the Incarnation passage and how it complicates and modifies the poem's main theme and narrative movement.

Clanness and *Cortayse* in the Incarnation Passage

The subject of the Incarnation passage is Christ, and especially his birth, but in this passage the events of Christ's life, including the Nativity, are not actually narrated as a story; rather, they are described and celebrated in a lyric of praise. Moreover, the saving events of Christ's death and resurrection are not even mentioned. This passage is thus not narrative, but rather a lyric meditation, and therefore it does not move the poem forward in time. Instead, the passage serves to change the point of view of the audience, to remind them that they have a radically different perspective on the poem's subjects: on "clanness," on sin and punishment, on their relationship to God, and on their hope for salvation. This perspective was hinted at in the Prologue, the only other part of the poem that works with the New Testament instead of the Old. The hopeful hints in the Prologue of humanity's invitation to God's presence are developed and strengthened in the Incarnation passage, which, unlike the Prologue with its technique of biblical paraphrase and commentary, works with poetic allusion and language play.

The Incarnation passage opens with the not uncommon suggestion of sexual romance as a metaphor for humanity's relationship to God. Though popular in many religious writings (especially lyric poems and mysticism), such a metaphor is nonetheless startling in a poem that stresses sexual purity. Furthermore, the poet does not merely speak of humanity's love for God as romantic (an analogy so commonplace as to carry little force), he even uses an overtly sexual word:

> If þou wyl dele *drwrye* with Dryȝtyn þenne,
> And lelly louy þy Lorde and His leef worþe,
> Þenne confourme þe to Kryst, and þe clene make.

> If you will have *a love affair* with the Lord then,
> And faithfully love your Lord and become his dear one,
> Then become like Christ, and make yourself clean.
>
> (1065–67; emphasis mine)[8]

The paradox of chastely loving God like a sexual lover is followed by the paradox of the Incarnation, described with a virtuoso play on images and words, especially "clene" (clean) and "clos" (closed, secret, enclosure). The Incarnation, we are told, is a pure taking on of flesh, a clean enclosing within a mortal body—"For non so clene of such a clos com neuer er þenne" (1088; For no one so clean had ever before come from such an enclosure)—and a clean breaking into an unviolated enclosure:

> For, loke, fro fyrst þat He lyȝt withinne þe lel mayden,
> By how comly a kest He watz clos þere,
> When venkkyst watz no vergynyté, ne vyolence maked,
> Bot much clener watz hir corse, God kynned þerinne.

> For see that from the first moment that he lay within the faithful maiden,
> By how lovely an arrangement he was there enclosed,

When no virginity was vanquished, no violence done,
But much cleaner was her body when God was conceived therein.
(1069–72)

The climactic paradox of this passage that keeps stressing both
the untouched purity and the passionate closeness of divine love finally
contradicts the poem's thesis that the unclean cannot enter the divine
presence:

And ȝif clanly He þenne com, ful cortays þerafter,
Þat alle þat longed to luþer ful lodly He hated,
By nobleye of His norture He nolde neuer towche
Oȝt þat watz vngoderly oþer ordure watz inne.
Ȝet comen lodly to þat Lede, as lazares monye,
Summe lepre, summe lome, and lomerande blynde,
Poysened and parlatyk, and pyned in fyres,
Drye folk and ydropike, and dede at þe laste,
Alle called on þat Cortayse and claymed His grace.

And if He came then cleanly, [He was] most courteous afterward.
All that belonged to evil He hated with loathing.
Out of the nobility of His nature, He would never touch
Anything that was vile or filthy inside.
Yet the loathsome came to that Lord—such as many wretches,
Some lepers, some cripples, and the halting blind,
Poisoned and paralytic, and suffering from inflammations,
Choleric kinds, and dropsical, and finally the dead—
All these called on that Courteous One and claimed His Grace.
(1089–97; emphasis mine)

The "ȝet" in the middle of these lines takes strong and abrupt exception
to God's hatred of uncleanness. The clue to that paradox is "cortayse,"
which mediates between "clannes" and "grace," between the preservation of pure holiness and the welcoming of all would-be followers,
between final irrevocable judgment and merciful forgiveness. In the
midst of this poem about "clannes," with its narratives of sexual, reli-

gious, and moral filth, narratives that place great stress upon the preservation of the pure and holy and the guarding against violation, we get an extended lyric meditation on Christ's *cortayse,* which apparently contradicts his *clannes.* Christ, who arrives "clanly" is "ful cortays þerafter"; his pure divinity becomes open, and "cortayse" is the word used by the poet to describe that openness.[9]

The "cortayse" that comes "þerafter" is exemplified in Christ's ministry, in his healing, in his institution of the Eucharist, and finally in his Passion and Resurrection. These last, the central historical events in Christ's life and in all history, are not recounted or even mentioned explicitly in *Cleanness,* but are only evoked implicitly through the reference to the Eucharist. As the description of Christ's breaking of the bread shows, although the Crucifixion seems the ultimate violence, it, like the Incarnation, is a pure, nonviolating act. Since the Eucharist is a reenactment of Christ's sacrifice, and the priest's act of breaking the bread in the Mass is a dramatic, visual symbol of the breaking of Christ's body, the poem's reference to Christ's breaking the bread refers simultaneously to the Crucifixion, the Last Supper, the Resurrection (the Supper at Emmaus, when the disciples recognized Christ "at the breaking of the bread," is one of the Resurrection appearances, recorded in Luke 24:13–35), and the Christian community's celebration of the Eucharist. The passage referring to the breaking of the bread emphasizes the "cleanness" of Christ's handling, so clean that he needs no knife or blade:

So clene watz His hondelying vche ordure hit schonied,
And þe gropying so goud of God and Man boþe,
Þat for fetys of His fyngeres fonded he neuer
Nauþer to cout ne to kerue with knyf ne wyth egge;

So clean was his handling that every bit of filth avoided it,
And so good was the touching of the one who was God and man both
That because of the skill of his fingers he never bothered
To cut, nor to carve with a knife, nor with a blade. (1101–1104)[10]

This breaking is a pure act; the divine is not corrupted by violation, but rather purifies the corrupt that it encounters, and it does so without intermediary or human assistance (without the use of knives).[11]

"Clanness" in *Cleanness*

By the time we come to the Incarnation passage we have a wide but
not especially complex, understanding of "clanness," the announced
topic of the poem. We have been told, implicitly and explicitly, that
"clanness" is a metaphor for virtue and obedience and godliness, but it is
also to be understood more literally, as the quality of sexual and physical
cleanliness—keeping oneself and God's creation pure and clean and
whole, unsullied by wrongful sex, improper union, corrupt or blasphemous language. Then, the final narrative, Belshazzar's Feast, adds to this
understanding by extending "clanness" to include ritual purity, the
respectful and proper use of sacred forms and objects, which it closely
connects with sexual purity, the proper use of a natural form. There is
thus an unexpected development in the meaning of the word *clanness,*
from the metaphorical, "spiritually free from sin," to the literal meaning,
"physically free from dirt or corrupt touching."

The poet begins by telling his audience that the clean garment they
need for God's feast is a virtuous life:

Wich arn þenne þy wedez þou wrappez þe inne,
Þat schal schewe hem so schene schrowde of þe best?
Hit arn þy werkez, wyterly, þat þou wroȝt hauez.

Which then are thy garments that thou should wrap thyself in,
Which ought to look like the very best and finest clothing?
They are thy deeds, certainly, that thou hast done.

(169–70)

Yet, from this straightforward though metaphorical use of its subject term,
the poem proceeds to make "clanness" more literal, to refer to the avoidance of pollution—not polluting God's creation with unnatural sex, like
that between the sons of God and the daughters of men, not corrupting
God's angels with "impure" food (leavened or salty) or with sodomy.

The Incarnation passage further adds a use that is at once flatly literal and very figurative—using *clene* to mean unbroken and inviolate,
whole and untouched—and then makes a complete reversal by insisting
on the unviolated wholeness of Mary's impregnated body and the purifying touch and healing of Christ, who will never touch filth and yet
heals the broken with his words and hands. Just as the Incarnation pas-

sage stands apart from the Old Testament tales in form and mode, so too its sense and use of *clanness* is quite different from the plainer and more common understanding of the term in the rest of the poem. Like the last stanza of *Pearl,* which similarly inverts many of that poem's previous assumptions, the Incarnation passage in *Cleanness* shows the divine presence no longer driven away by the *contraré* of *clanness,* but rather converting it and purifying it. In one sense, Christ, as represented in the Incarnation passage, is less present than the God who speaks to Noah and whose interior monologue is reported to us, and who confesses to Abraham his great sorrow at the abuse his gift of sexual love has suffered (697–710). But the Christ of the Incarnation passage is at the same time nearer than the God who only communicates through the mysterious signs in Belshazzar's Feast, and he is certainly more approachable than the angry God who sends flood and fire to destroy his filthy creatures.

The Incarnation passage's more hopeful view of God, as well as its more complicated and less severe understanding of "clanness," is literally buried among the tales of divine wrath and punishment and enclosed within the framing story of God's increasing distance from humanity. In the main narrative frame God's presence becomes an absence, graced only by the hope and desire for the beatific vision; in place of a present reality his people are given a future possiblity. No longer able to hear his voice, they long for the end of time when they will "se þat Semly in sete and His swete face" (1055; see that Lovely One enthroned and [see] His sweet face). In the meantime, the poem's readers are enjoined to be clean and pure, the virtues required in most apocalyptic texts and in any view that sees this world as dirty, corrupt, and ungodly and the deity as distant and angry. The story of *Cleanness* is the story of how humanity has brought itself to this apocalyptic mode, or rather of how they had brought themselves there, until the unique event, the coming of Christ, which is beyond the time of *Cleanness*'s stories and therefore not recounted, the event that was to reverse the distancing of the divine. The importance of that untold event is underscored by the stories and framing narrative that are told—stories with dark and forbidding implications that burden their poet and that stand at the outer edge of his other, far brighter, and more hopeful poems.

Chapter Four
Patience

Patience tells the story of Jonah, who is swallowed by a whale when he tries to escape his mission to preach to Nineveh. This is the shortest of the Pearl poet's poems and in many ways the most accessible and the most likeable. Despite this and the fact that *Patience* has some features in common with *Sir Gawain and the Green Knight*—both tell well-structured stories centering on a single protagonist—-readers tend to group *Patience* with the poet's other two explicitly religious and biblical poems, *Pearl* and *Cleanness*. However, *Patience* is easier to read than either of its predecessors in the manuscript: it is shorter and tells a more engaging story. Furthermore, unlike *Pearl*, *Patience* is relatively free of theology and exegesis, and its lively narrative is far easier to follow than *Pearl*'s intricate versification. *Patience* is more "realistic" (in the sense that it is closer to everyday life) than the first two poems in the manuscript, its protagonist is more engaging and more recognizable, and its dialogue is more lifelike (even though it is largely a dialogue between a mortal and God, much of it conducted from inside the belly of a whale). Jonah's story is more immediate, more present, what many would call "more relevant" to us as readers than that of either the Jeweller in *Pearl* or the protagonists in *Cleanness*'s several narratives.

Moreover, while *Patience* shares with *Cleanness* a reliance on the Bible for its stories—drawing from the Old Testament for the main narrative and the New Testament for an introduction—these two poems are markedly different in important ways: first, in contrast to *Cleanness*'s group of stories, *Patience* focuses on one story and one protagonist, which results in a tighter narrative structure and a more detailed and sympathetic portrayal of the main character; and second, *Patience* has a more hopeful, less forbidding worldview than *Cleanness*. In addition, although it has gone largely unnoticed, I believe both poems are responding to an apocalyptic mood and tone, such as characterized much of the art and literature of late medieval England. The responses of the two poems are different, however, though their differences are more complementary than contradictory. *Cleanness* sounds a note of doom, barely relieved by hope, while *Patience*, though fully acknowledging humanity's weakness and deserved damnation, takes a more forgiving attitude toward God's creatures and ends by promising mercy. With the exception of Nebuchadnezzar, Sarah, and Lot's Wife, the people in *Cleanness* are either thoroughly good, like Noah, or hopelessly wicked, like the Sodomites. In *Patience,* in contrast, we have wicked Ninevites, who repent, and a God-fearing prophet, who repeatedly errs.

Most of the criticism of *Patience,* both in book-length studies of the Pearl poet and in the relatively few separate studies of this poem, has proved more valuable than much of what has been written about *Pearl* and *Cleanness*. *Patience* has, in fact, been more accessible to everyone: scholars, critics, and students. While a few readers focus on the allegorical and figural significance of Jonah's story, most concentrate on the poem's more mimetic features and on its plot and character.[1] In fact, Schleusener, who, quite rightly I believe, argues for the centrality of history and action in this poem, says that the poet "does not make a great deal of Jonah's figural status."[2] Spearing writes especially well about the engaging and down-to-earth humor of Jonah's speech and characterization, while Davenport has given us a fine analysis of Jonah's change of heart in the belly of the whale and of how the poet has adapted his biblical source to make this conversion clearer.[3] The poem's explicit theme of "patience" is the topic of Elizabeth Kirk's valuable essay "'Who Suffreth More Than God?': Narrative Redefinition of Patience in *Patience* and *Piers Plowman*."[4] Kirk shows that the kind of patience the poet redefines is stronger and much more active than the rather weak definitions we tend to have for the virtue of patience today. As useful as some of the small body of criticism on *Patience* has been, however, it tends to be unusually specialized, and no one has tried to join the several approaches together. Even Kirk's essay, insightful as it is, is not concerned with the poem as a whole, let alone with its connections to the poet's other works.

However, I believe that analysis of the virtue of patience can be usefully joined to the critical work on the poem's realism and its historical action. In *Patience* the poet's redefinition of the word *patience* involves playing with the word, just as he does with the central words in *Cleanness* and in *Pearl,* and again this playfulness tends to focus on and to reify the signifier. However, in *Patience* the Pearl poet does not separate the signifier from its meanings, which remain important to the way we read the poem. In fact, by the end of this poem the signifier and the signified, that is, the term "patience" and its various meanings, come together as a reality that has an active role in history and in the lives of the audience, not just in texts and exegesis.

Patience and the Apocalyptic Mode

Thus, in *Patience,* as in *Cleanness,* the poet has used his thematic term in a way directly linked to the poem's view of salvation history. We have seen that *Cleanness* focuses on types of the End and adopts for the most part an apocalyptic view of history and of God's relationship to humanity, and that its central virtue, cleanness, is the one appropriate to the apocalyptic mode: wholeness as holiness; and ritual, physical, and sexual purity—these are the qualities that separate the saved remnant from the corruption and filth of fallen creation. Patience, on the other hand, is the virtue urged in the different, more hopeful view of history presented in *Patience.* For, as I have argued previously, this poem, while primarily set in pre-Incarnation time, works against the chief features of apocalypticism: the dark view of sinful and irredeemable humanity and an angry punishing God; the focus on the Last Days, which looks to future, divinely wrought catastrophes to destroy evil and to restore good; the distance of God, who communicates primarily through written messages and obscure signs; and the resulting need for scribes and interpreters instead of patriarchs and prophets.[5] Read together, *Cleanness* and *Patience* provide a full and balanced commentary about sacred history and God's relationship to his creation. While acknowledging the appeal of the apocalyptic mode, the Pearl poet finally seems to abjure not only its obsessive concern with sin and punishment, but even more its dark view of history and humanity. Jonah, like both Gawain and the Dreamer in *Pearl,* is weak and fallible, but he is far from the irredeemably sinful "bad guys" in *Cleanness.* Jonah is thus more human than any characters in *Cleanness,* and interestingly enough, so is God. In *Patience* God is not a distant, terrifying judge, but a loving, if often nagging and scolding, father. Here God's presence is strong, both for his prophet Jonah and for all those to whom God speaks through his prophet. Above all, *Patience* asserts the reality and the primacy of God's presence and the central role of prophets, who reveal the divine presence in the spoken word.

This last difference, God's presence as opposed to his distance, is directly related to the two different comments the respective poems, *Cleanness* and *Patience,* make about the apocalyptic mode. *Cleanness* reveals both the causes for apocalypticism—humanity's moral filth and God's absence from this world—and the longing such a mode reflects. *Patience,* in contrast, moves beyond the apocalyptic mode to the prophetic mode, which is marked by a hope for reconciliation. This hope involves enlarging the pattern of judgment so that it becomes a pattern of conversion. Unlike *Cleanness, Patience* does not show God's revulsion at and distance from humanity, but rather records his continuous involvment with his creation. Jonah cannot escape God, even though he tries more than once to do so. The different views of God and of the pattern of providential history that are reflected in *Cleanness* and *Patience,* respectively, account for the different roles of the patriarchs and the apocalyptic seer in *Cleanness,* on the one hand, and of Jonah as prophet, on the other. The patriarchs in *Cleanness* follow orders from God in carrying out his judgments, while the seer Daniel functions, as we have seen, essentially as an observer of historical events and an interpreter of the written word. But prophets like Jonah work *in* history, with both God and his people. They hear and speak God's words, and they work as agents of conversion, not as instruments of judgment. Furthermore, the audience of *Patience* (like the readers of the Book of Jonah) are included in the prophet's audience—they are addressed by him, and through him they hear God's word. In *Patience* this inclusion comes partly through the audience's involvement in Jonah's fortunes and misfortunes.

This closeness of the audience to the poem is, I believe, a result of the poet's deliberate strategy to bring the world and the time of the poem into the present and to move beyond both the pastness of the past and the distance of the future. The Pearl poet effects this change in a variety of ways: by his choice of biblical texts, by the structure of his narrative, and finally by a tour-de-force rhetorical ploy at the end of his poem. To see how the poet actually manages this move into the present and how this movement is related to the thematic virtue of patience, it is necessary to trace the poem's structure and plot and to examine closely the poet's narrative strategies, especially his choice of and use of biblical texts. But before addressing those topics, I want to make a few comments about the early church's views of history, since these views have bearing on the respective New Testament texts used as Prologues for *Patience* and *Cleanness.*

The early Christian church was much concerned with the *eschaton,* the promised end to this world and time. Both Jesus's preaching (as found in the Gospels) and that of his disciples (as reflected in Acts and in the Epistles) refer repeatedly to the imminent end of history. Indeed, it is fairly clear that most early Christians expected the end momentarily, certainly within their own lifetimes, for this is what Jesus and his followers seem to promise. However, although some events occurred that looked like the "Last Things," notably the Fall of Jerusalem in A.D. 70, history and time did not stop as expected.

The longer the Day of the Lord was delayed, the more awkward the church's position became. It is this problem that is addressed in the Second Epistle of Peter, in a passage that is explicity relevant to *Patience*:[6]

> The present heavens and earth are reserved by God's word for fire.
> They are kept for the day of judgment, the day when godless men
>   will be destroyed.
> This point must not be overlooked, dear friends.
> In the Lord's eyes, one day is like a thousand years and a thousand
>   years are like one day.
> *The Lord does not delay* in keeping his promise—though some
>   consider it "delay."
> Rather, he *acts patiently,* since he wants none to perish, but all to
>   come to repentance.
>
> (*Non tardat Dominus* promissi,
> sed *patienter agit* propter vos nolens aliquos perire,
> sed omnes ad paenitentiam reverti.)
>
> The day of the Lord will come like a thief,
> And on that day the heavens will disappear with a roar; the elements
>   will be destroyed by fire,
> And the earth and all its deeds will be made manifest.
> . . . .
> Truly we await new heavens and a new earth, where, according to
>   his promise, the justice of God will reside.
>
> (2 Pet. 3:7–10, 13)[7]

In this passage the apparent conflict between God's desire for the conversion of sinners and his inevitable judgment and punishment of evil is resolved by His patience. The end will eventually come, the judgment will then be final, and the evil cast out forever, but in the meantime God waits patiently. He endures the history of humanity's repeated failures, and His endurance is not passive inaction or a failure to intervene, but paradoxically an *act of patience*.[8]

The problem raised in this passage from the Petrine epistle is crucial to the understanding of *Patience* and indeed has bearing upon the Book of Jonah too. *Patience,* in recounting the story of Jonah, presents us with a very fallible prophet, one who is wrong thinking as well as wrong acting. Jonah has a tendency to focus on the end of history and to see any postponement of apocalyptic destruction as delay. Jonah also is inclined to take divine signs for human signs that are susceptible to his own manipulation and misinterpretation; he uses God's signs, whether pattern or word or visual image, as finite human ones. For example, Jonah acknowledges God as Creator of the earth, but then expects that Creator to be confined to one locale. Furthermore, while Jonah looks ahead to purifying acts of divine judgment, he seems unwilling to acknowledge humanity's own responsibility for reform and repentance.

The lesson for Jonah, and for the poem's audience, is to stop concentrating on the distant apocalypse and instead to bring God's kingdom into the present—and thus paradoxically to go one step beyond apocalypse. Going beyond apocalypse involves moving away from the linearity of an eschatological perspective and replacing the linear pattern of judgment with the circular and open-ended pattern of conversion. The paradox of going beyond the eschaton, which is to redefine the end, is closely connected to the paradox embodied in patience and to what Kirk calls the poem's "narrative redefinition of patience," a redefinition that amounts to tranforming patience from a human term or sign to a divine one. The poet's definition and use of patience make it an active virtue, a divine quality that characterizes not just God's long sufferance but also his involvement in human history. By extension, patience becomes the virtue best suited to God's servants and prophets in "the middest," those who must work within history, who must cease looking to a distant, timeless future and become instead responsive to the present reality of God and his will.[9] For Jonah, having finally delivered God's warning, becomes furious when Nineveh is spared from threatened destruction. In the Bible the prophet regrets God's well-known patience and mercy (Jon. 4:2); in *Patience* the poet has added to Jonah's complaint words that specifically accuse God of delay, in a remarkable echo of the argument of the Petrine epistle:

Wel knew I Þi cortaysye, Þy quoynt soffraunce,
Þy bounté of debonerté and Þy bene grace,
Þy *longe abydyng* wyth lur, Þy *late* vengaunce.

I well knew thy courtesy, thy wise sufferance,
Thy bounty of graciousness, and thy good grace,
Thy *long endurance* of harm, thy *delayed* vengeance.
                              (417–19; emphasis mine)

From the beginning of the poem the Pearl poet sets the stage for this complaint of Jonah's about the delayed eschaton, so that by the time Jonah makes it, we as readers can recognize his error, for, as 2 Peter tells us, "God does not delay."

The Prologue

I would like now to trace the way the poet sets this stage and how he develops the issue of God's patience and his seeming delay. The poet begins with the Beatitudes, a New Testament text remarkable in its implicit comments on both the eschaton and its relevance to the audience's lives. Like the Parable of the Wedding Feast that introduces the Old Testament stories in *Cleanness,* the Beatitudes are concerned with the kingdom of God, but they give a very different view of that kingdom. The parable in *Cleanness* focuses on judgment: who is included in, who excluded from, the kingdom. The Beatitudes, in contrast, describe the bliss of that kingdom: what life there will be like, and what its members will be like. However, many readers of the Bible, as well as of *Patience,* have not realized how central the kingdom of God is to the Beatitudes. In both medieval and modern readings the Beatitudes are usually seen as a set of rules to live by. But, as has also been noted, the demands of the Beatitudes far exceed most social guidelines, as well as the rules of Mosaic law. In fact, the Beatitudes do not so much prescribe behavior, as describe it, and moreover what they describe is actually the kingdom of God, though not a mythic, future reign, but one realizable now within each of Jesus' followers. In other words, the Beatitudes stand in sharp contrast both to the visions and images of future bliss provided in John's Apocalypse and also to the idea of an external, public, that is, earthly, messianic kingdom obedient to Mosaic law. Unlike the signs of God's kingdom referred to or described in *Pearl* and *Cleanness,* which are highly visual images like God enthroned or the New Jerusalem, the Beatitudes (in both Matthew's longer and Luke's shorter versions) deemphasize the visual image of heavenly joy by focusing on the abstract, internal quality of blessedness that characterizes the kingdom of God.

In addition, the Beatitudes are placed in a frame of present time, thereby undercutting some of the suggestions of a distant visionary future. The first and last Beatitudes, which specifically promise the kingdom of God, assert the present reality of the kingdom for those who are "poor in spirit" and who endure persecution:

> Blessed are the poor in spirit for theirs *is* the kingdom of Heaven.
>
> . . . .
>
> Blessed are those who endure persecution for justice's sake for theirs
>   *is* the kingdom of Heaven.
>
> (Matt. 5:3, 10; emphasis added)

Unlike the other Beatitudes, all of which promise a future happiness, such as the promise that those who weep "shall be comforted" (Matt. 5:4), the first and last Beatitudes give their promise in the present tense. The contrast between verb tenses and the resulting emphasis on the present reality for the poor in spirit and those who suffer persecution is retained by the Pearl poet in his version:

> Thay are happen þat han in hert pouerté,
> For hores *is* þe heuen-ryche to holde for euer;
>
> . . . .
>
> Thay ar happen also þat for her harme wepes,
> For þay *schal* comfort encroche in kythes ful mony;
>
> . . . .
>
> Þay ar happen also þat con her hert stere,
> For hores *is* þe heuen-ryche, *as I er sayde.*

> They are blessed who have poverty in their hearts,
> For theirs *is* the kingdom of heaven to have forever;
>
> . . . .
>
> They are blessed also who weep for their troubles,
> For they *shall* gain comfort in many lands;
>
> . . . .
>
> They are blessed also who can control their hearts,
> For theirs *is* the kingdom of heaven, *as I said before.*
>
> (13–14, 17–18, 27–28; emphasis mine)

The use of the present tense, by both Matthew and the Pearl poet, makes it clear that this is no mythic kingdom, no conventional paradise or New Jerusalem, but an internal state, one that is not visualized, but is fully realized. To make sure we do not miss the connection between the first and last Beatitudes, the Pearl poet has added the reminder "as I said before" after the last Beatitude; and further he tells us afterward:

> For in þe tyxte þere þyse two arn in teme layde,
> Hit arn fettled *in on forme,* þe forme and þe laste,
> And by quest of her quoyntyse enquylen on mede.

> For in the text where these two are laid out as a subject,
> They are joined *in one form,* the first and the last,
> And through pursuit of their wisdom earn one reward.
> (37–39; emphasis mine)

Although there has been little agreement among scholars about how to translate "fettled in on forme," and particularly what is meant by "on forme," I am convinced that the phrase refers first and foremost to the grammatical form, the use of the present tense as opposed to the future tense, that joins together the first and last Beatitudes. By extension, these two Beatitudes are of the same form in a more figural sense, because they promise the same blessing and because they involve the same virtue.[10] As the poet tells us, "in myn vpynyoun, hit arn of on kynde" (40; in my opinion they are of one and the same kind). The poor in spirit and those who suffer persecution are alike in their patience and they are blessed with the "heuen-ryche." More precisely, they do not *gain* the kingdom of God—they already have it within them.

Not only is the kingdom of God thus made a present reality, it is internalized. In contrast to the highly visual images of heaven provided in *Pearl* and *Cleanness,* the "heuen-ryche" of *Patience* is abstract and distinctly nonvisual. The subsequent exegesis offered in the Prologue to *Patience* picks up on this non-visual quality and resorts to personifying the virtues in order to emphasize the internalization of the kingdom. "Pouert" and "Pacyence" (Poverty and Patience), two of the "ladies" of the Beatitudes (30–33) are seen as the narrator's "playferes" (45; companions), and his reluctant submission to their presence is an allegory of the proper conditioning of his heart. The personification allegory mode is rare for this poet and is used here, I believe, in order to emphasize the internalization of the blessedness of the Beatitudes.

The Story of Jonah

Following the Prologue, *Patience* demonstrates in its narratives that the opportunity to enjoy the kingdom of God now is inseparable from humanity's responsibility in salvation history. Unlike the apocalyptic focus on God's final and future acts of judgment, purification, and redemption, Jonah's mission to Nineveh exemplifies what humanity can do by undertaking its own conversion rather than awaiting God's judgmental action. This moral and doctrinal revision parallels the poem's revision in narrative structure, from the linear and closed to the circular and open. As God adjusts Jonah's thinking about judgment and action, mercy and patience, so also he adjusts Jonah's and the reader's views of history. A providential plan does not mean a simple straight line, which is the limited narrative structure of the stories within *Cleanness,* and a promised end does not mean a foregone conclusion.

The story of Jonah, both in the Bible and in *Patience,* comprises three linked narratives of conversion: the major one is the story of Jonah himself; the other two are the story of Nineveh and the story of the sailors. Jonah's story contains some of the most unusual features of a conversion narrative and is the most complex and most significant plot in *Patience.* However, before turning to Jonah himself, we should look first at the Ninevites' and the sailors' stories, in order to distinguish the basic pattern of a conversion narrative in its simpler forms.

In *Patience* we learn that the people of Nineveh have fallen into wicked ways; they are full of "vilanye and venym" (71; villainy and venom) and are not behaving in accord with God's plan. God then takes the first action and sends his prophet to warn Nineveh of divine vengeance. Nineveh responds by embarking on a full-scale program of repentance. Led by their king, all the Ninevites, including the animals, do penance. God then, "Þaʒ He oþer bihyʒt" (408; although he promised otherwise), withholds his vengeance.

The story of the Ninevites illustrates that the purpose of God's Word is to save and restore his creatures, not to destroy them; the other two narratives make even clearer how much this act of restoration involves God's patience and how it apparently delays the promised end. The story of the sailors' conversion is less impressive than the complete turn-

ing to God by the Ninevites. To begin with, the sailors are not introduced to us as a wicked people; moreover, in their lack of knowledge
regarding God's plan, they seem more neutral and less guilty than the
Ninevites. On the other hand, unlike the Ninevites, the sailors do not
respond immediately when Jonah tells them about the true God. At
first, they ignore the Word of God spoken by his prophet and bend even
more energetically to their rowing. When they do finally respond to the
message with a patient acceptance, then their ship is saved and their
story has a happy ending.

In the story of Jonah himself we find two special features not found in
the Ninevites' or in the sailors' narratives: Jonah's story is individualized
and internalized, and it is open-ended. Although Jonah's narrative has
what could be a "happy ending," it does not end there, but goes on to a
conclusion that for many (including Jonah himself) lacks finality and is
anticlimactic. Both the internalization and the open-endedness of
Jonah's conversion allow us to witness the continuing progress of salvation history and the corresponding divine patience required in such a
pattern. One way of viewing Jonah's development is as a reeducation in
salvation history, "reeducation" because all along Jonah betrays a knowledge of God and his purposes without, however, accepting the full implications of such knowledge. Jonah first recalls God's roles as sovereign
and creator; later he learns the full extent, through time and space, of
the Creator's power and loving concern; finally, Jonah is taught the lesson, stressed in the Petrine epistle, that the Lord does not want his creatures to perish, but to be restored to him (2 Pet. 3:9).

Jonah's conversion involves a gradual change of heart, one that has
psychological plausibility as well as dramatic suspense, both of which
have been traced in detail by certain critics (Spearing 1970, 83–88, and
Davenport 119–30).[11] In following this development, we as readers are
brought close to Jonah's experience and become involved with him in
ways that we do not with any of the characters of either *Cleanness* or
Pearl. At the same time, we are kept at a certain distance from Jonah,
especially when he is behaving foolishly and willfully. The poet's rhetorical strategy for creating both empathy and distance is the fairly common one of ironic humor. As Spearing points out, we laugh at Jonah
when he is a fool, and we sympathize, albeit with a smile, when he is in
trouble (Spearing 1970, 83).

In order to realize this double purpose of empathy and distance, the
Pearl poet has added to his biblical source. Some of these additions rationalize Jonah's behavior and make his experiences more vivid, while oth-

ers comment upon that behavior and those experiences, so that we are more aware than Jonah of the larger picture—of where his story fits into God's plan and of its implications for us as audience. We understand better than Jonah does that he is only one of many, that his role as a prophet must be subsumed in the overall plan of Providence, and, finally, that the neat and tidy conclusiveness of a closed narrative is not the pattern of salvation history.

One example of how the poet rationalizes Jonah's behavior is the account of Jonah's escape into Nineveh, which is flatly reported in one verse in the Book of Jonah (1:3), but expanded into 56 lines in *Patience*. In this expansion the poet narrates Jonah's thinking process: first, his fear that when he preaches to Nineveh he will be attacked and imprisoned for bearing bad news (the proverbial case of punishing the messenger on account of the message); second, his resulting decision to flee from God; and third, his darkly humorous self-pity, when he thinks that God does not care about him, that the Lord above just sits on his throne, and would not give thought to poor Jonah, even were he suffering on a cross. The poet also adds, with his usual lively and mimetic "pointing," a description of the ship setting sail.[12] All these additions explain and make vivid Jonah's escape. At the same time, this well-realized and dramatized episode of Jonah's flight is punctuated with narratorial comments, sometimes in the exegetical voice of a preacher citing other scriptural evidence, sometimes in the more familiar voice of a parent scolding a naughty child. These comments provide an ironic distance since they allow the poem's readers a larger view than that held by Jonah.

The poet's additions to his source in this passage serve a third purpose: providing figural significance. Several figural signs are invoked when Jonah grumbles:

> "Oure Syre syttes," he says, "on sege so hyȝe
> In His glowande glorye and gloumbes ful lyttel
> Þaȝ I be nummen in Nunniue and naked dispoyled,
> On rode rwly torent with rybaudes mony."

> "Our Lord sits," he says, "on a throne so high
> In His shining glory, and cares very little
> Whether I were seized in Nineveh and stripped naked,
> And pitifully torn apart on a cross by villains."

>   (93–96)

First, this is the most explicit allusion in the poem to the traditional "Sign of Jonah," a favorite sign for the early church of Christ's suffering, death, and Resurrection, a sign first mentioned by Jesus himself in Matthew's Gospel (12:39–40). Second, in this reference the sign of Christ's death is combined with the image of God on his throne, an image primarily drawn from John's Apocalypse and its immediate Old Testament sources, and an image much used in the Middle Ages: it was sculpted on doorways to churches, depicted in mosaics and stained glass, and reproduced on a smaller scale in ivory book covers and manuscript illustrations. Furthermore, the two signs, Christ suffering and God the Father reigning above, have been joined into one: an image of Christ hanging on the cross with the face of God the Father above, usually in a heavenly cloud. This particular version, often with the Holy Ghost as a dove flying down between the Father and Son, was reproduced often in the Pearl poet's time, in English alabasters and manuscript pictures, and so would no doubt have been familiar to the poet's audience.

The poet's invocation of the figural significance is more complicated than simply pointing to Jonah as a Christ figure. In fact, as I have already indicated, I believe that in *Patience* Jonah's figural status is large-ly undercut.[13] What Jonah's indirect reference to the Sign of Jonah does is remind the audience of the larger frame of salvation history, while making it clear that Jonah cannot see this pattern, except in a self-absorbed, and therefore twisted, way. Jonah knows the sign of Christ on the cross (an anachronism, of course),[14] and he sees himself in that role, but not as, to use the Apostle Paul's words, "obediently accepting even death, death on a cross" (Phil. 2:8), rather as a self-pitying prophet, abandoned by his Father. In fact, Jonah does not even really acknowl-edge that God is his father, for it is the poet who calls God "father"—in the preceding line, whereas Jonah refers to God only as "Our Lord" (line 92; compare line 93). Meanwhile, the audience should know not only that the Crucified One has willingly chosen to suffer, but also that the reigning God is watching over all with great care and concern. In case the audience misses the irony, the poet makes it explicit much later when Jonah is swallowed by the whale and is to all appearances drowning: "Bot he watz sokored by þat Syre þat syttes so hi3e" (261; But he was succoured by that Lord who sits so high), preserved by that same reign-ing Lord whom Jonah believes "gloumbes ful lyttel" (94; worries very little—*gloumbes* literally means "frowns"; the best translation for this phrase would probably be the more idiomatic "doesn't give a damn").

A similar expansion and rationalization of the biblical text comes with Jonah's sojourn in the whale. Here, however, the poet concentrates his efforts on the mimetic realization of Jonah's experience. As Spearing puts it, "the grotesque vigour" of the description of the whale's interior is combined with "the quiet and exact irony of 'Ther watz bylded his bour, that wyl no bale suffer' [276; there was a home built for the one who would not endure any trouble]" (Spearing 1970, 84–85; my translation). One minute we are with Jonah, slipping and sliding through the whale's slimy guts, and the next we are brought up short (not unlike Jonah when he "blunt[s] in a blok as brod as a halle" (272; stops abruptly in a compartment as big as a hall), reminded both of God's loving concern and Jonah's willful rebellion. The occasional ironic detachment of the comments, together with the farcical aspects of the mimetic re-creation of Jonah's experience, serve to deflect the figural association with Christ's death.

The largest and most important change the Pearl poet makes at this point in Jonah's story is to give him a long prayer in the whale, a prayer that serves to rationalize his subsequent speech. The biblical text here has always been problematic, since the oft-quoted passage known as the "Jonah Psalm" (2:3–10) seems not to fit the occasion or the events. In this psalm Jonah speaks in the past tense of being "cast into the deep" (2:4) and of crying out to the Lord and being answered (2:3); then later Jonah says that God "brought up [his] life from the pit" (2:7). But Jonah was thrown into the sea not by God, but by the sailors, and he did not sink into the depths, but was instead immediately swallowed by a whale.[15] Most inconsistent of all is the statement that Jonah cried out to the Lord, since there is no mention of his ever doing such a thing. Some modern biblical commentators provide a simple, if not very satisfying, explanation for the inconsistency: the psalm is an earlier and separate composition, imperfectly inserted in the story of Jonah at a later date.

Since medieval Christians believed the Bible to be written under divine inspiration, such an explanation would not be available to the Pearl poet, and, in any event, it is not much help in understanding Jonah, even for modern readers. Therefore, to solve the problems created by the Jonah Psalm, what the poet has done instead is to provide Jonah with an earlier speech, a penitential prayer that asks God for mercy and rescue.[16] In this first speech Jonah acknowledges both his faithlessness and his foolishness, as well as God's omnipotence "on land and sea" (288), and begs for mercy. Immediately the worst of Jonah's discomfort ends. He no longer slips and slides through the whale's disgusting guts, but finds a relatively cozy resting place, "saf for merk one" (except for darkness only; in other words, the only exception to his improved situation is that it is still dark). Then the poet expands on Jonah's change of heart, by telling us that Jonah spent three days and three nights meditating on God's "might" and "mercy" and "fairness" (295), and only after this meditation does the poet have Jonah speak what is called a "prayer" (303). The psalm or prayer, as the poet gives it, is a close Middle English paraphrase of the Jonah Psalm in the Bible, with a small but critical change: where Jonah states in the Bible that the abyss surrounds him, the poet has him say that the waters are around "þe body þat I byde inne" (318; the body in which I abide, that is, the whale).[17] I mention this small change as evidence of the pains the poet has taken to make sense of Jonah's psalm of thanksgiving. The most important difference in this regard is, of course, the addition of the earlier prayer, which eliminates the inconsistency in the biblical text of having Jonah refer to a plea that has not been mentioned, let alone recorded.

At the same time, the poet's changes make adjustments in the allegorical significances of Jonah's sojourn in the whale, deflecting references to Christ's Passion and strengthening those to every mortal's death. The Sign of Jonah itself has traditionally contained both of these meanings. In particular, the Jonah psalm, with its personal expression of suffering, represents the anguish of everyone facing death or any terrible ordeal. Christian teaching, from Paul on, has always stressed the idea that each follower of Christ must be ready to share in Jesus' death in order to share in his Resurrection (see especially Rom. 6:3–4).[18] Thus Jonah's three days and three nights in the belly of the whale prefigure not only Christ's death, but everyman's. It is this latter allegorical reading (what would be the tropological, or moral, one) that is most at work in *Patience*. The mimetic details of the whale's belly, which bring us close to Jonah's experience, at one and the same time deflect the references to Christ (who can hardly be pictured in this farcical routine of pratfalls) and also emphasize those to everyman. Moreover, by adding the first prayer and thereby rationalizing the Jonah Psalm, the poet brings us close to the steps of Jonah's conversion. In bringing his audience near to Jonah's experience, the poet involves them in salvation history and simultaneously moves that part of history into the present. At the same time, because some ironic distance is maintained between the reader and Jonah, the reader is more conscious than Jonah of the full implications of his experience, not just the suffering to be endured in dying, but also the resurrection that is to follow.

There is one other important rhetorical strategy that the Pearl poet uses for dramatizing and interpreting Jonah's experiences: the use of parallel motifs or scenes that invite comparison and contrast. In this poem the parallel motifs are Jonah's three different hiding places, one each to each of three main episodes in his story: his escape into Tarshish, his sojourn in the whale, and his sulky retreat under the woodbine (notably, there is no retreat for the one remaining episode in the Book of Jonah—during the preaching to Nineveh—because this is the one place in his story when Jonah is fully participating in salvation history). We should note that, whereas the Bible contains two of these retreats—the one during the storm and the one under the woodbine—the Book of Jonah makes no mention of any special hiding place in the whale. By adding the retreat in the whale, the poet invites us to compare and contrast two very different kinds of solitude: alone *away from* God, and alone *with* God. The first hiding place, the one on shipboard, is an extension of the flight itself. First, Jonah tries to flee from God and his mission to preach to Nineveh, and then, when God pursues him with a storm, the reluctant prophet runs away again by hiding in the bottom of the boat. Curled up there, while the sailors above are desperately trying to save their ship, Jonah "slypped vpon a sloumbe-selepe, and sloberande he routes" (186; slipped into a deep sleep and snores with a slobber—note the alliteration). This onomatopoeic line, which mimics and describes the vulgar sound associated with deep slumber, also alludes to the traditional interpretation of Jonah's sleep in the boat. Jerome, for example, likens Jonah's sleep to that of the Apostles in the Garden of Gethsemane, both of which typify "torpid man in the deep sleep of sin" (*Patrologiae* 25, col. 1179; translation mine). The secret little corner in the boat, the deep sleep, and the flight on shipboard are all signs of Jonah's withdrawal from God and from God's plan.

Similarly, in the woodbine episode, Jonah "slydez on a sloumbe-slep sloghe vnder leues" (466; slides into a deep, slothful sleep under leaves), in what is not just a similar situation but also a close verbal parallel to the earlier line. As on shipboard, sleep under the woodbine comes as the final act in a series of Jonah's movements away from God: first, verbally grumbling and threatening suicide (413–28); second, physically withdrawing from Nineveh "on est half of þe hyʒe place" (434; on the eastern side of the city, literally, the high place); and finally, literally building his own world, a "bour" (bower), completely enclosed, with only a "nos on þe norþ syde" (451; a little opening, literally a "nose," on the north side),[19] where Jonah can once again hide from God, this time from God's loving mercy toward Nineveh, as earlier he hid from God's command to preach to Nineveh.

Each of these two retreats, the one in the boat and the one under the woodbine, is based on the biblical account, and their similarities are straightforward, fairly obvious, and traditional in biblical exegesis. To them, the poet has added a third retreat, the one inside the whale. This third parallel is superficially like the other two because it includes a hiding place and because Jonah is alone. Otherwise this is a hiding place of a very different kind: it is not *away from* God, but *with* God, and it is not of *Jonah's* making but of *God's* making, and in it Jonah does not sleep. To ensure that we see the parallel, the poet makes an explicit comparison between this "hyrne" (hidden corner) in the whale and the earlier one on the ship:

> As in þe bulk of þe bote þer he byfore sleped.
> So in a bouel of þat best he bidez on lyue.
>
> As in the bottom of the boat, where he had slept before,
> So in the bowel of that beast he stays alive.
>
> (292–93)

Yet, in the whale's "hyrne" Jonah does not sleep, much less snore. Rather, here he spends "þre dayes and þre nyȝt, ay þenkande on Dryȝtyn" (294; three days and three nights, ever thinking on the Lord). From this meditation comes Jonah's second prayer, which, as we have seen, provides a rational and explicit explanation for Jonah's conversion inside the whale. In other words, although Jonah is alone in the whale and not actively pursuing God's plan, he is not asleep, not slothful, not removed from God, but rather turning toward both God and his mission. It is all the more striking, then, that the poet would draw comparisons from the sojourn in the whale to Jonah's other hiding places, explicitly to the one on shipboard and implicitly to the woodbine shelter. A "hyrne" in God's protection is thus likened to the ungodly actions of deliberate disobedience and willful removal from God's kingdom. In addition, Jonah's safe retreat within the whale is enclosed in darkness, universally a sign of God's absence.

By so drawing attention to the paradoxically hellish and sinful qualities of this union with God, the poet undercuts the reliability of visual and sensory signs. He thus directs our attention, as he does in the Prologue, to the inner quality of God's kingdom. In *Patience* holiness, union with God, safety, comfort, and joy are abstract, inner qualities, not visually perceived paradises or mythic realms of jewel-bedecked cities. Jonah's experience in the whale has become a lonely encounter with suffering and with God, an experience that is available to all (as journeys to the underworld or excursions inside a whale's guts are not).

The Role of Patience in Salvation History

In *Patience* the poet makes vivid Jonah's progressive conversion. As the audience is brought closer to Jonah, so too the story is made more familiar and more present. All of this allows the poet to strengthen his message that everyone's role, like Jonah's, is to participate patiently in God's plan. Sometimes that participation involves an active role like preaching, and sometimes it demands the more passive role of abiding in prayer alone with God, but never is it to be confused with passive inaction, even though it may look outwardly the same. In addition to illustrating the difference between Jonah's impatient inaction and his patient abiding, the poet develops his theme of active patience through God's behavior. For, as several critics have pointed out, God, not Jonah, is the exemplar of patience in this story (for example, Spearing 1970, 77–78). God's patient action takes two forms in *Patience*: the action of pursuing sinners, of threatening them with destruction if need be; and the action (which looks like inaction to some humans) of awaiting the conversion of those who have strayed and of forgiving the contrite. This second patient action, waiting, has a direct effect on the narrative pattern of salvation history: it causes a delay, or, more accurately, a postponement of the conclusion. Thus the story of Jonah does not end with the destruction of a city (as does the story of Sodom and Gomorrah or of Belshazzar's Feast), nor does it conclude with the Ninevites' conversion, as does the sailors' story in the Book of Jonah. Rather, Jonah's story continues into the seemingly anticlimactic episode of the woodbine. This part of the narrative illustrates, both in its actual subject (God's decision to spare Nineveh) and in its narrative structure (the postponement of the conclusion), that salvation history is open-ended and contingent. For mortals "in the middest" the end can only be a future vision, not a present, let alone a past, reality.[20]

The open-endedness and the inconclusiveness, which are inherent in the biblical story, are made stronger in *Patience,* which ends with a move into the present time of the poet and his audience. The poet effects this

move with an artful manipulation of voices in the last lines, to which I now
turn, for they make the clearest statement about the role of patience in salvation history for both God and his creatures. At the close of the poem,
after reminding Jonah of the divine love for creation by comparing it to
Jonah's fondness for his woodbine, God contrasts Jonah's "hastif" (520;
hasty) judgment with God's "mercy" (523). Then follow these lines:

> Be noȝt so gryndel, godman, bot go forth þy wayes,
> Be preue and be pacient in payne and in joye;
> For he þat is to rakel to renden his cloþez
> Mot efte sitte with more vnsounde to sewe hem togeder.

> Be not so angry, good man, but go on your way.
> Be steady and patient in pain and in joy;
> For he that is so hasty as to tear up his clothes
> Must afterward be stuck with even more trouble in sewing them
>   together.

(524–27)

These lines present problems for editors and readers. The questions are:
Is this still God speaking? Where does his voice stop and the narrator's
take over? Andrew and Waldron give the best solution: while God is
speaking until this point (through line 523), the next four lines (the
ones quoted above) form a "bridge" to the final lines of the poem,
which are, as all agree, in the narrator's voice (Andrew and Waldron,
206, note to line 524).[21] The voice that we hear in the poem's closing
lines, the same voice found in the Prologue, is thus a personal voice
speaking directly to us:

> Forþy when pouerté me enprecez and paynez innoȝe
> Ful softly with suffraunce saȝttel me bihouez;
> Forþy penaunce and payne topreue hit in syȝt
> Þat pacience is a nobel poynt, þaȝ hit displese ofte.

Amen.

> Therefore when poverty and much pain oppress me,
> Very gently must I be reconciled with sufferance;

For penance and grief prove this full clearly:
That patience is a noble matter, though it displeases often.
Amen.
(528–31)

The "bridge," the lines between the conclusion of God's speech and the beginning of the narrator's, is the prophetic voice that appears in Isaiah, Jeremiah, and in virtually all the prophets, including the Book of Jonah, the voice that puts God's Word in the mouth of the prophet and that is usually introduced with the phrase, "Thus says the Lord."[22] The poet, by merging the narrator's voice with God's and by conflating historical past time with present poem time, does for his poem what is urged in the Prologue: he moves into present time and internalizes the kingdom of God.

The poet has thus not only redefined patience in his poem, from a weak, passive virtue to an active one, from endurance to participation; he has himself been a patient actor, a poet who has brought God and his voice within, fitted his story into salvation history, and accepted contingency and inconclusiveness. He has recounted a story in order to bring us not to an end but to a beginning and more precisely to a present time, moving out of Old Testament history into the "present" time of the poet and his audience, where they must await patiently the return of God's kingdom.

Chapter Five

Sir Gawain and the Green Knight

Sir Gawain and the Green Knight, the last poem in the manuscript, is by far the best known and the most popular of the poet's works. A romance tale combining various Celtic and folk motifs with traditions about King Arthur and his knights, *Sir Gawain and the Green Knight* recounts Gawain's adventures after he accepts a challenge to play a beheading game with a gigantic green man. This poem is unique among the Pearl poet's works, set apart from the other three by both its secular subject and romance form.

Since its rediscovery in the mid-nineteenth century, this poem has been the subject of enormous scholarly and critical study. Because of this great wealth of material, much of which is available either directly through critical essay collections or indirectly through introductions to the many editions of the poem, I will not attempt to give a general view of the criticism of *Gawain.*[1] Instead, I will mention a few of the most prominent approaches to the poem and then go on to concentrate on the aspect that I consider most important, especially for the new reader: the poem's genre as Arthurian romance. After discussing the assumptions and conventions that belong to the romance genre, I will examine how the poet works with them, adapts them, and sometimes subverts them. In addition, because the poet's particular version of the romance genre is strongly affected by his versification, style, and language play, I will, as with my discussion of the other poems, look very closely at some key passages that I find particularly revealing of the larger questions of form and genre related to *Gawain.*

One approach to this poem that I will not be using must be mentioned, since a student is likely to meet with examples of it, namely, the exegetical or Robertsonian method—"exegetical" because it is what medieval exegetes, that is, interpreters of the Bible, did; or "Robertsonian" after its first and most famous proponent, D. W. Robertson, Jr. Critics of this school allegorize the poem, looking for its Christian and moral themes, for, as they point out, medieval readers were especially inclined to read texts in this way. There is no doubt that moralizing a story, whether classical or medieval, has always been popular in Western literature, but it has never been, even in the Middle Ages, the *only* way to read a poem. An overly allegorical reading tends, I believe, to reduce a poem to a not very engaging sermon. In the process, exegesis removes a poem's language play, its versification, its poetic figures, its wit and humor—in short, many of the qualities that make *Sir Gawain and the Green Knight* such a brilliant and successful poem.

Very different from the Robertsonian method, but in my view similar to it in its reliance on materials outside the poem, is much of the most recent criticism, especially feminist, cultural, and the so-called new historicist criticism. These approaches also "allegorize" the poem, but not to find its religious message; instead, they extract morals about oppression and analyze the relationships between women and men, rulers and ruled, and rich and poor. Certainly, a courtly romance like *Sir Gawain and the Green Knight* must be somewhat concerned with the various relationships in a court, as well as with those between men and women, and therefore some of the criticism that focuses on such aspects of the poem can be revealing. However, all too often critics of these schools resort to a reductive moralizing tendency that lacks even the historical authenticity of the Robertsonian approach.

Moreover, some romances, *Gawain* in particular, seem less suited to many of these politicizing methods. As Muscatine first observed, the Pearl poet seems to be "a man for whom the perfection of his art has become a kind of defense against crisis,"[2] for he generally seems to avoid political issues, both those of gender and those of power. Whereas certain romances (Béroul's *Tristan,* for example) depict court gossip and intrigue, the Pearl poet's romance shows little interest in such matters. With one exception, courtiers in *Gawain,* whether at Camelot or at Hautdesert, tend to act as a unit and seem univocally loyal to their respective lords, Arthur and Bertilak.

Although relationships among nobles or between the lord and his vassals do not figure much in the Pearl poet's romance, those between men and women do. The role of women in *Gawain* is somewhat unusual for a courtly romance, since the hero is not in love with any lady: the only lady he serves is the Virgin Mary and the only lady he talks to is paying court to *him,* rather than the reverse. These gender issues have been the subject of some recent and interesting feminist criticism. Probably the most useful is Sheila Fisher's article, "Leaving Morgan Aside."[3] Fisher's thesis is that the real power behind the romance is Morgan and its major active player is Bertilak's lady (notably never given a name), but that these women have been marginalized and displaced by the lesser, usurping, male players: Gawain, Bertilak, and King Arthur. While Fisher's argument is not without a certain validity, I find its usefulness in helping us read the poem limited. It is worth remembering that the one explicit piece of evidence for Morgan's role, Bertilak's testimony at the end of the poem, could be read in several ways, rather than at "face value," as Fisher apparently does.

One study that does yet another kind of cultural analysis, R. A. Shoaf's *The Poem as Green Girdle: Commercium in "Sir Gawain and the Green Knight,"* discusses the poem in economic and commercial terms.[4] Shoaf's analysis is especially appropriate, since, as Shoaf puts it, "the commercial vocabulary of *Sir Gawain* consistently informs its structure" (2), and since the poem was written at a time of "unprecedented economic upheaval" in England (11). However, I think Shoaf's approach is not very useful as an introduction to the poem. Studies like Shoaf's require more knowledge, both of economic history in the fourteenth century and of the traditions in Christianity concerning commerce and exchange, than nonspecialists are likely to have, and are therefore best suited to advanced study of the poem.

Sooner or later almost all critical approaches, new and old, are involved with an analysis of Gawain and his role. In fact, it is a natural tendency in the average reader, not just now but in the Pearl poet's time as well, to look closely at the hero and his development. There are dangers with this approach, of course—different ones according to the precise assumptions about human psychology and fictional characters that one brings to an analysis of the hero. While Robertson and members of his school tend to reduce all of Gawain's actions to *caritas* versus *cupiditas,* and the new historicists and the feminists reduce the hero's actions to power struggles, other readers are inclined to look at Gawain's development as though he could be analyzed psychologically. Certainly, Gawain should be a major focus of the reader's interest. However, he is neither a character in a novel nor an allegorical figure in a sermon, but instead a figure in a romance, with a long history as a leading knight in earlier Arthurian romances. We will therefore not properly appreciate Gawain's role until we first understand what a romance is, recognizing that the romancier owes different allegiances to other literary traditions and assumes an audience with different expectations than the novelist. Reading *Gawain* in terms of its genre as romance is thus central, and even essential to its interpretation, especially for the new reader.

Sir Gawain and the Green Knight and the Genre of Romance

What, then, is a medieval romance? What are its features and expectations? How should we read a romance—more precisely, how should we read it, as opposed to how we read an epic, or a novel, or a lyric poem, or a short story? A fine and succinct description of a medieval romance, particularly of the courtly kind, can be found in *Sir Gawain and the Green Knight* itself. This description is provided by the Lady of Hautdesert, who tells Gawain:

And of alle cheualry to chose, þe chef þyng alosed
Is þe lel layk of luf, þe lettrure of armes;
For to telle of þis teuelyng of þis trwe knyȝtez,
Hit is þe tytelet token and tyxt of her werkkez
How ledez for her lele luf hor lyuez han auntered,
Endured for her drury dulful stoundez,
And after wenged with her walour and voyded her care
And broȝt blysse into boure with bountées hor awen—

And in the whole of chivalry, the thing most praised
Is the loyal pursuit of love, the code of warfare;
For, to speak of the endeavors of true knights,
It is the title and text of their works,
How lords have ventured their lives for their true loves,
Suffered dreadful hardships for the sake of their love,
And afterward avenged themselves through their valor and
    dispelled their pain,
And brought bliss into their [probably the ladies'] chamber with
    their [the knights'] achievements.

(1512–19)

Although she uses the term "chivalry" instead of "romance," the Lady is clearly speaking not just of chivalry itself, but even more of the stories about chivalry, namely, those found in chivalric romance.[5] According to the Lady, these stories are about war and love and also about the knights who practice both the "lel layk of luf" and "þe lettrure of armes." Love and arms are a common pair in courtly romance; Chrétien de Troyes, for example, uses the paired terms "courtoisie" and "proesce."[6] *Courtoisie,* or "courtesy," includes the art of love, but is a more general term referring to the sophisticated gentility—good manners and fine speech, for example—of the cultural elite. "Courtoisie" thus embraces the values of a more civilized, more "feminine," culture. *Proesce,* literally "prowess," refers both to the knight's honor and the actual achievements that establish that honor—his skills as a fighter on horseback, his courage and integrity—-all the values of a masculine, warrior culture.

The Lady in *Sir Gawain and the Green Knight* is taking her paired (and easily contradictory) sets of values and placing the emphasis on the courtly, gentility side, making a knight's achievements as a warrior depend upon his duty as a lover. In many ways the Lady's definition of romance fits the common assumptions we hold today. Most of us think of a "romance" as a story with a happy ending: a story about young knights and their ladies; a story set in a fairytale world, one in which there are magical happenings taking place in a setting free of political or social contexts, geneological backgrounds, or geographical or historical precision and accuracy.

There are, however, a few ways in which the Lady's description differs from what someone might give today or what we can infer from other medieval romances. One aspect of the Lady's description that would not be common today is her reference to love as a game. (Although I have translated *layk* as "pursuit," the word, which comes from the Old Norse *laikr* [to play], more precisely means "amusement" or "playing."[7]) In addition, the Lady does not speak of warfare in itself, but of the "lettrure" of warfare, the learning or perhaps code of warfare—the word *lettrure* specifically connotes written learning. Moreover, the Lady's whole definition is very literary: it is the "title" and the "text" of the knights' "werkkez" that she describes.[8] She thus subsumes a knight's deeds of arms and his suffering for love all within the language of literature, and she speaks of knights as if she were a reader of romances, even though she herself is a character within a romance. This conflation of romance actions with romantic tales is common in courtly romances, where *aventure* (adventure), is the word both for an event or a series of events and also for the story of those events. *Werkkez* in the Lady's definition serves a similar double purpose, for it can mean both "works" as deeds and "works" as written texts (particularly in the sense of constructed or designed literary creations).

The kind of literature that the Lady in *Sir Gawain and the Green Knight* is talking about is the courtly romance that focuses on love and on the arts of "courtoisie." The Lady's perspective is appropriate since she belongs to a sophisticated court, but she has, in fact, omitted many aspects of other Middle English romances, especially those about Arthur and his knights. She seems to be unconcerned about historical events and indeed to view Gawain purely as a literary personage. For the medieval reader, however, Gawain is not just a fictional character, but one from history—if not actual history, at least legendary history. Historical figures who inhabit a romance carry an authority and a validity that purely fictional characters do not. On the other hand, with certain quite interesting exceptions, romances handle these figures not so much as the subject of historical studies, but rather as the source of a set of cultural values. This is admittedly a fine distinction, and there are romances that center so much on the world and time of a legendary figure or event—on Alexander the Great or the Trojan war, for example—that we can only say they are different from history because they are not historical (a circular argument of the kind that bedevils generic theory).[9]

The Arthurian romances are the most important and most obvious example of this mixture of history with romance, especially in medieval England. (The so-called *romans d'antiquités* [romances of classical antiquity] were also very popular.) As far as we know, the first history to mention Arthur explicitly, giving him the name "Arthur," and to present him as a king of Britain, was Geoffrey of Monmouth's *History of the Kings of Britain.* This work has always held a dubious position as history, despite its title and despite its claims to authenticity through its use of Latin and of a supposed written source. Although English poets and dramatists looked to Geoffrey's *History* for its good stories about England's monarchs (Shakespeare used it as a source, for example), from early times many historians have condemned Geoffrey as a liar and a fraud.[10] Certainly, Geoffrey's chapters on King Arthur read more like romance than history, for they remind us of the pretty, fairytale-like world of medieval knights and their ladies, the world of Chrétien de Troyes, Spenser's *Faerie Queen,* T. H. White's *Sword in the Stone,* Lodge's *Small World,* and all those awful, and therefore unmentionable, romances that crowd airport bookstores.

On the other hand, some Arthurian romances work quite hard to be "nonromantic," concentrating on the authenticity of their stories and the historical implications of their events. Two notable prose compilations, the Vulgate cycle, written in thirteenth-century French, and Malory's works, composed in English in the fifteenth century, are the most important and best known of these kinds of romances. Although works like these are not without magic elements, love affairs, and the various trappings of romances, they lay claim to telling a "true story," and they usually take pains to set their stories in some kind of historical context. Malory, for example, gives details both of King Arthur's parentage and birth and also of his death and the loss of his kingdom, thus providing a perspective on Arthur's role and on his place in Britain's history.

Composed before Malory but after the Vulgate cycle, *Sir Gawain and the Green Knight* is contemporary with two English Arthurian romances that also exhibit a historicizing tendency: the *Stanzaic Morte Arthure* and the *Alliterative Morte Arthure*. These two verse narratives focus on Arthur himself, not on one or more of his knights, and more particularly, as their titles indicate, they tell of the troubles and wars that marked the end of Arthur's kingdom and that are the subject of the final parts of the two prose compilations, the Vulgate cycle and Malory's works.

One obvious explanation for this interest in Arthur's kingdom and its fall was the growing consciousness in late medieval England that its land and culture should be separated from the continent of Europe.[11] From Geoffrey of Monmouth on, one senses in English romances and histories an emerging need for the English to define themselves, to claim an *English* history and an *English* identity, a need caused precisely because so much of their political history since 1066 had been merged with that of France and so much of their culture borrowed directly from French and other continental sources and traditions. In other words, if late medieval England's history, language, literature, philosophy, and art had been more truly "English" or "British" and less Western European (whether Latin or Norman French), then presumably English writers of the fourteenth and fifteenth centuries would not have gone to so much trouble to claim (or reclaim) Arthur for their own.

It is no doubt also significant that the same texts that attribute the fall of King Arthur's kingdom, either wholly or in part, to Lancelot's adultery with Guinevere usually identify Lancelot as French. Gawain, on the other hand, was traditionally held to be of northern English or Scottish stock and predictably seems to have been preferred by English romanciers—he certainly is a favorite hero of shorter English romances and lais (for example, *The Wedding of Sir Gawain and Dame Ragnell,* or *Sir Gawain and the Carl of Carlisle*).[12] One cannot push this kind of interpretation too far, of course. The Vulgate cycle, for example, is of French origins and written in French, but it carefully and exhaustively traces the unhappy consequences of Lancelot's love for Guinevere from its very beginning to the disastrous battle on Salisbury Plain, a battle lost primarily because King Arthur has been in France warring against Lancelot's family. On the other hand, most readers of the Vulgate cycle find Lancelot a sympathetic figure. By the end of the last book of the cycle, *The Death of King Arthur,* Gawain has replaced Lancelot as the major source of Arthur's problems, for it is Gawain's continued anger that forces Arthur to pursue Lancelot and his brothers to the Continent. In contrast to Gawain, Lancelot tries to make peace with King Arthur and Gawain's family and ends his days as a holy hermit, doing penance for his sins. This view of Gawain's role in the downfall of Arthur's kingdom became a strong enough tradition to be carried over into the later English accounts, but in them Gawain's culpability is usually softened; and alongside this tradition England produced many tales and romances glorifying Gawain.

About the same time that England was beginning to produce its own "Englished" versions of the Arthurian romances, we also find other romances, concerned either with legendary English heroes like Bevis of Hampton or with historical ones like Richard Coeur de Lion. Some of these romances, Bevis of Hampton and Guy of Warwick, for example, exist in several versions, thirteenth-century Anglo-Norman texts and later English ones (around 1300 for Bevis and Guy).[13] According to Crane, "[C]entral to all these works is the English hero's status as fictional forebear and defender of his nation" (54).

Certainly, not all English romances, even the later ones, show this historicizing and anglicizing tendency, nor are all of them popularized tales, whether about local, legendary heroes or about Arthur or his knights. Some of the later English romances are closer to the courtly romances from France, the ones that the Lady of Hautdesert seems to have been reading, which focus on an individual knight and his feats of prowess and his love affairs. A few of these are directly based on courtly French romances, such as the Middle English *Ywain and Gawain,* an adaptation of Chrétien's *Yvain.* For most of us, however, even these Middle English romances lack the intensity and introspection of the French romances' devotion to the abstract issues surrounding chivalry. For the most part, as Ganim and others have argued, the Middle English romancier is more concerned with telling a good story and getting on with the events than with spending time examining the implications of those events.

Certainly, the English poems (and presumably their audiences) are less courtly, less self-conscious about poetic craft, less sophisticated, and less artful, and have a decidedly less French setting than their continental predecessors. Few Middle English romances, for example, include the Norman-French terms for courtly pursuits and topics such as heraldry and hunting, even though these terms were still in actual use in England well past the fourteenth century. Moreover, the heroes of the later Middle English romances indulge in fewer interior monologues and appear less refined and less aristocratic than Chrétien's heroes. Likewise, the fairies and magic of these Middle English tales seem less magical, less wondrous, more everyday, and more ordinary and English.[14]

All of these noncourtly characteristics have earned Middle English romances the label "bourgeois"—although that is an adjective that probably raises more questions than it answers. A better term is "popular," for these romances definitely have a more popular feeling to them than their continental predecessors.[15] As Burrow and others have shown, most Middle English romances suggest a setting in which a minstral or tale-teller spins a good story to an audience of many kinds of people, not just to a court consisting of the literary and cultural elite. Without getting into the scholarly debate about oral origins or composition of some of these Middle English romances (and recognizing that those we read today have obviously survived as written texts), we can still believe, as Burrow has argued in *Ricardian Poetry,* that within most Middle English romances there is at least a literary pretense that we are listening to an oral poet or reciter—there is what Ganim calls a "consciousness of an addressed public" (151).[16] (Whether that pretense was once a reality probably can never be proved, and anyway the question, though intriguing, is not relevant here.)

Sir Gawain and the Green Knight is no exception in this regard, since, especially with its beginning, it creates the sense of a storyteller reciting a tale to a present audience. However, the few touches of the English popular romance found in *Gawain* coexist with features of other kinds of medieval romance. Like most courtly romances, this poem focuses its attention on an individual knight and structures its story in the form of the hero's quest. But the Pearl poet does make his romance more typically English by choosing an indisputably English hero and by setting his tale in the context of English history. At the same time, along with the poem's features of the popular tale, the poet includes references to written authority that are more characteristic of the historicized prose romances.

The unique mixture of different kinds of romance found in *Sir Gawain and the Green Knight* is most evident in the opening stanzas.[17] The poem begins with its most "historical" lines:

> Siþen þe sege and þe assaut watz sesed at Troye,
> Þe borȝ brittened and brent to brondez and askez,
> . . . .
> Hit watz Ennias þe athel and his highe kynde,
> Þat siþen depreced prouinces, and patrounes bicome
> Welneȝe of al þe wele in þe west iles.
> . . . .
> And fer ouer þe French flod, Felix Brutus
> On mony bonkkes ful brode Bretayn he settez
>   Wyth wynne,
>   Where werre and wrake and wonder
>   Bi syþez hatz wont þerinne
>   And oft boþe blysse and blunder
>   Ful skete hatz skyfted synne.

> After the siege and the attack at Troy was ended
> And the city left ruined and burnt to ashes and cinders,
> . . . .
> It was the prince Aeneas and his noble family,
> Who afterward conquered lands, and became rulers
> Of almost all the wealth in the western realms.
> . . . .
> And Blessed Brutus, far across the French sea [the English Channel]
> On many wide shores, he establishes Britain,
>   With joy,
>   Where war and strife and strange events,
>   By turns, have followed there,
>   And often both joy and sorrow
>   Have quickly taken their turns.
>   (1–2, 5–7, 13–19)

This opening places the poem in an explicitly British setting. Arthur is a British king, one of a long line of rulers descended from their founding father, Brutus.

However, the sense of history belongs more to legend than to written chronicles. For example, whereas the tradition that Aeneas's descendent Brutus founded Britain is a common one (originating in the historians Eusebius and Nennius),[18] it is hardly authoritative and factual, even for the Middle Ages; it is more the stuff of romance histories than of chronicles and written records. Moreover, the last lines of *Gawain*'s opening stanza, which make up the rhyming quatrain of short lines called the "wheel," treat time and history as a series of cyclical events rather than as precise moments in a linear chronology. This wheel serves as a transition to the second stanza, in which the poet moves even further into the vaguer time and space of romance. We are given no specific historical place for King Arthur, but rather are told:

Ande quen þis Bretayn watz bigged bi þis burn rych
Bolde bredden þerinne, baret þat lofden.
. . . .
Bot of alle þat here bult of Bretaygne kynges
Ay watz Arthur þe hendest, as I haf herde telle.

And when this Britain was built by this noble warrior,
Stout men, who loved fighting, arose there.
. . . .
But of all the kings of Britain who resided here
Arthur ever was the noblest, as I have heard tell.
(20–21, 25–26)

Moreover, the sense of a chronological background of historical Britain has been replaced by the mode of fairytales and popular minstrelsy:

Forþi an aunter in erde I attle to schawe,
Þat a selly in siȝt summe men hit holden
And an outtrage awenture of Arthurez wonderez.

If ʒe wyl lysten þis laye bot on littel quile,
I schal telle hit astit, as I in toun herde,
            With tonge.
      As hit is stad and stoken
      In stori stif and stronge,
      With lel lettres loken,
      In londe so hatz ben longe.

And so an adventure on earth I intend to set forth,
Which some people consider a wondrous thing to behold,
And an extraordinary adventure among Arthur's wonders.
If you will listen for just a little while,
As I heard [it told] around, I shall tell it right now,
            Aloud.
      As it is set down and recorded
      In a tale brave and strong,
      With true letters joined,
      As it has long been [known] in [this] land.

                                                    (27–36)

Possibly, the phrase "lel lettres loken" actually refers to the metrical art of
alliteration, but even if it is just a phrase equivalent to "well-turned" or "put
together with true words," this preamble still promises a well-told tale (or
"laye") to those who listen, even as it cites the authority of tradition.[19]

The movement toward romance is completed when the poet begins his
actual story. Set in Camelot, the story begins with a sumptuous feast
attended by well-known figures from Arthurian tradition, who are busy
flirting and playing various courtly holiday games. Arthur, the young and
energetic king, "sumquat childgered" (86; somewhat childlike/boyish),[20] is
equally gay and playful. Rather than doing kingly things like waging wars
or arbitrating disputes or granting favors, Arthur is waiting for a bit of
adventure before he eats (a custom that is mentioned in other romances),[21]
waiting to have presented to him "sum auenturus þyng, an vncouþe tale /
Of sum mayn meruayle" (93–94; some adventurous thing, a strange tale
of a great marvel), a story about princes, arms, or other adventures. This
marvelous thing that King Arthur awaits does not have to be an actual

event: it could be a challenge from a knight (96–97), but it could also be just a story of a marvel, in keeping with romance's tendency to conflate event and the record of an event into one *aventure.*

With the stage set for a marvel, a marvel duly appears, with a climactic effect brilliantly re-created by the poet. First, there is "anoþer noyse ful newe" (132; another noise quite new), warning court and audience that something is about to happen. Then the strange knight enters: riding his horse right into the feast hall (incidentally, a not uncommon happening in romance), he is a startling creature, huge yet elegant. With expert use of his verse form, the poet saves the most crucial information about this uninvited guest until the wheel at the end of the stanza:

> For wonder of his hwe men hade,
> Set in his semblaunt sene;
> He ferde as freke were fade,
> And oueral enker grene.
>
> And men wondered at his color,
> Clearly seen in his appearance.
> He behaved like a knight that was bold[?],
> And [was] bright green all over.
>
> (147–50)

We further learn that the Green Knight is richly arrayed in gold and green and carries no sword; instead, in one hand he bears an axe with intricate carvings and trim, and, in the other hand a holly bob—the latter presumably a sign of peace and of the Christmas season. At this point we still do not know the creature's purpose, much less his identity; like the narrator, who withholds the information about his color, the Green Knight himself creates suspense for court and reader by postponing the announcement of his challenge.

The narrator and the court view the Green Knight with mixed responses to these various and sometimes contradictory signals. The narrator, for example, practically stutters in his initial hesitancy over whether this is a giant or a human:

> Half-etayn in erde I hope þat he were,
> Bot mon most I algate mynn hym to bene,
> And þat þe myriest in his muckel þat myȝt ride.

> A semigiant on earth I suppose that he was,
> But at any rate the largest man I consider him to have been,
> And the most pleasing of his size that ever did ride. (140–42)

King Arthur, equally unsure of this knight's identity or purpose, first greets him as a guest and invites him to join their feast. Then, when the Green Knight says he does not plan to linger but has instead come to test the fame of the court, Arthur understandably assumes a challenge to battle is being offered (this is one of the adventures customarily expected at a feast [see lines 96–98]). Not so, says the Green Knight, since here there are only unworthy opponents—mere "berdlez chylder" (280; beardless children). Instead of combat or jousting, the Green Knight seeks only a game. But this game turns out to be more dangerous than actual fighting, for the Green Knight proposes a Beheading Game—an exchange of blows in an attempt to decapitate the opponent. The suggested "game" so horrifies the court that they are stunned into silence, until King Arthur, embarrassed by his knights' hesitation and by the Green Knight's derisive laughter, steps forth to take the challenge himself. It is clear from both the knights' and the king's responses that not only is the proposed game deadly serious, but it bears important implications for the reputation of the Arthurian court. The movement here is important: we have been taken from a courtly feast with merry games, to a startling and magical appearance, back to a courtly feast, then briefly to the possibility of battle, and again back to feast and play, but with a new mood of horror, for the earlier kissing games and the present giving have been replaced by a risky, indeed potentially fatal game that constitutes a challenge to the honor of King Arthur and his knights.

The alternation of game and laughter with horror and serious danger continues throughout this opening scene. For example, in tones of deadly seriousness, but with a bit of smiling understatement, King Arthur advises Gawain to strike well, so there will be no chance of a return blow. Later, there are touches of farce, as well as horror, when the decapitated head is kicked around like a football and even more when it terrifyingly, but also ludicrously, looks to Guenevere and speaks, commanding Gawain to keep his appointment. The effect, similar to that of horror movies or ghost stories and many fairytales, is a pleasant shiver of terror, rather than genuine dread. Jonassen believes that the poet creates "a tension beween frivolous game and life-and-death seriousness" and that the Green Knight "is both a playful organizer of games and a purveyor of death."[22] It is evident that the Green Knight's

visit has caused uneasiness when King Arthur goes to such trouble to
reassure everyone, Guinevere in particular, that this horrific adventure is
all part of the holiday festivities. As soon as the Green Knight leaves,
Arthur says:

"Wel bycommes such craft vpon Cristmasse—
Laykyng of enterludez, to laȝe and to syng—
Among þise kynde caroles of knyȝtez and ladyez."

"Well-suited are such doings at Christmas time—
Performing of plays, laughing and singing—
In the midst of these seasonal carols of [sung by] knights and
    ladies."

                                                                  (471–73)

Throughout the rest of the poem there are similar mixtures of sophisticated games and uncouth terrors. For the most part, the games and
sophistication remain inside, in castles where lords and ladies play and
feast, whereas outside, especially well outside in the wilderness, lurk
threats of giants and other wild creatures. But this dichotomy is not only
breached when one of those wild creatures intrudes into the courtly gaiety
of Camelot at Christmastime, it also breaks down in the very person of the
Green Knight himself, who, as we have seen, combines elegance with
uncouthness. The poet, in fact, has carefully constructed his poem in a system of parallels and contrasts, which at once both maintain the separation
of courtliness and otherworldliness and also challenge that separation.[23]
    This set of parallels and contrasts not only applies to the figures and
motifs, it also organizes the plot. The story begins and ends in the court
of Camelot, the archetype of courtliness, where laughter and game and
good manners rule. Set against Camelot is the wilderness Gawain must
travel through on his quest, and especially the Green Chapel, which
turns out not to be a Christian place of worship, as its name, but not its
resident Green Knight, would suggest—this is at best a lonely and at
worst a terrifying world. Similarly, the two games that organize the plot
apparently fit the courtly/uncouth classification. The Beheading
Game—whether from Celtic tales, as most have assumed, or owing
more to the Mummers' Play, as Jonassen argues—frames the story in
grotesque danger. This game is begun by the Green Knight in the hor-

rific scene at Camelot, and it concludes at the Green Chapel in an atmosphere of fairy, even satanic, terrors.

The second game, which organizes the events in between, is played at a court, and involves the noble pursuits of hunting and "luftalkyng" (literally, "lovetalking," that is, talking of and with love). In the Beheading Game we have talking heads, the omnious whirr of an axe being sharpened, and a general atmosphere of otherworldly terror. In the Exchange-of-Winnings Game, in contrast, we have the carefully observed rules of the hunting game (for which by the fourteenth century there were a number of treatises covering everything from terminology to the notes for horn signals to the proper way to "undo" the prey) paired with the elaborate courtesy of gracious flirtation that masks a serious seduction attempt.

However, since the Green Knight, who institutes the first, otherworldly game, turns out to be none other than Bertilak of Hautdesert, the host who proposes the courtly Exchange-of-Winnings Game, the division does not hold, any more than wild green creatures can be counted on to remain in their wild green countryside. Moreover, it is Bertilak, the Green Knight in his other persona, who pursues the courtly game of hunting according to the rules, and his own lady who engages in the sophisticated seduction of the hero. The poet has constructed this part of the story as a particularly elaborate set of parallels, with three days of hunting and flirtation, which the narrator moves between with far more adroitness than usually found in the "meanwhile back at the castle" kinds of plot structure common in many romances with more than one story line. And yet the careful structure is belied by the increasing conflation of the two motifs: Bertilak's hunts become gradually less rule-bound, and the Lady's seduction grows less genteel and more threatening. On the third day the hunt for the fox has many hints of moral language and virtually no suggestion of manly dangers or skills, while the Lady's flirtation with Gawain has become morally dangerous, and very like a hunt in its pursuit of the prey.

There is thus much of game, much of magic, much of love in Gawain's adventures. What there is virtually none of are the deeds of arms associated with chivalry, much less any major battles or wars or conquests of kingdoms. Nor is there any reference during Gawain's quest to the larger context of British history, or even to Arthur's place in it. Only at the poem's close, after Gawain has returned to Camelot and related his adventure amid laughter and general acclaim (despite his own personal shame), does the poet return to the world of British history, now authenticated even more, with the written authority of the "þe best boke of romaunce" (2521; the finest book of romance), and the "Brutus bokez" (Brutus chronicles) that "bere[s] wyttenesse" (2523; bear witness) to the stories of King Arthur.

The very last lines, with their prayer to Christ (the one who wears the crown of thorns), add another note of seriousness, one more authoritative than written chronicles. While no such explicitly Christian reference appears in the poem's opening, some are scattered throughout the main story at various points, especially in the bedroom scenes, where the game gradually takes on a moral seriousness, even an overtly Christian one. Gawain himself is repeatedly presented as a Christian knight, embodying Christian virtues and devoted to the Virgin Mary, whose image appears on the inside of his shield. In many ways the occasional references to Christian morality are typical of chivalric romance and the general context of their values. Certainly, Gawain's Christianity often seems but part of his chivalric trappings—it goes with the image, so to speak. For example, when Gawain is alone in the wilderness and longing for a haven, he worries about keeping the "costes" (750; customs) of his religious observances. Moreover, the sign of the pentangle, which exemplifies the Christian cast to Gawain's chivalric virtues, is not mentioned again after the narrator's initial lengthy description and explanation. Unlike the Grail romances, which keep their spiritual message well in the foreground, the Pearl poet's romance makes specifically Christian references only sporadically.

Except for the concluding prayer, these Christian references all concern Gawain: his behavior, his fears, his needs, his guilt. Gawain is thus not just the subject of the romance, but a kind of measuring rod of its tone and attitude, and an indicator of how the poem works as a romance and what comments it makes upon chivalric values. When we laugh at or with Gawain, the romance is lighthearted and comic; when we struggle with judging Gawain's adventures and actions, the story takes on a mood of moral seriousness. Gawain's strengths and successes serve to redeem chivalric values, while his failures call them into question. I would like now to look closely at the figure of Gawain, in order to analyze further the craft and message of the poem.

The Role and Figure of Gawain

During the course of his story we see Gawain change from a humble, loyal member of Arthur's family and court, to a knight alone on a quest, to a much-feted guest at Hautdesert, to an embarrassed penitent at the Green Chapel. Each of these roles is characteristic of a certain kind of romance, though it is unusual to find them all combined in one hero in a relatively short narrative. By the end, when he returns to Camelot, Gawain seems to fulfill virtually all of his different roles at the same time, according to the point of view: his own, the court's, or the narrator's.

When we first see Gawain in action, when he steps forward to beg King Arthur for the right to play the Beheading Game, his manner epitomizes the humble, loyal knight. Claiming no other privilege or right than his family relationship to Arthur and the fact that he is the first to ask, Gawain even says that he is the "wakkest" (weakest) and "of wyt feblest" (354; least smart) of the knights.

Despite the explicit humility of Gawain's speech here, his claims to fame are clear. First, the blood relationship is no small matter. For, in fact, the relationship of maternal uncle to nephew is a privileged one in both custom and literary tradition.[24] Second, Gawain indirectly reminds everyone that he alone has behaved as the loyal vassal who fights on behalf of his lord, since it is "not semly" (348; improper) for the lord to fight when "mony so bolde yow aboute vpon bench sytten" (351; so many bold warriors are seated on benches around you), even though, as the narrator has already indicated, these same bold warriors have not made a move (see especially 241–49 and 301–2). Third, Gawain boasts of both King Arthur's prowess and that of his knights, who "vnder heuen I hope non haȝerer of wylle / Ne better bodyes on bent þer baret is rered" (352–53; under heaven, I believe, none are fitter of spirit nor stronger of body on the fields where battle is waged). Finally, in what are some difficult lines for readers and editors, Gawain may be assertively looking to the rest of the court for support in his request:

"And syþen þis note is so nys þat noȝt hit yow falles,
And I haue frayned hit at yow fyrst, foldez hit to me,
And if I carp not comlyly let alle þis cort rych
      Bout blame."

"And since this maxtter is so foolish that it ought not to fall to you,
And since I have requested it from you first, grant it to me,
And if I do not speak fittingly, let the whole court [say so]
      Without offence."

(358–61)

Gawain's elaborately courteous speech is thus not a sign of his unworthiness, but rather part of the game of courtliness and one more proof of his qualifications as the ideal Arthurian knight, which is then verified by his prowess in decapitating the Green Knight with a single blow.

The focus of the story has now shifted from Arthur and his court to Gawain. Similarly, despite the untowardness of the appointment (not a conventional single combat) and Arthur's efforts to treat the matter as a Christmas game, Gawain's promise to seek out the Green Knight at his mysterious Green Chapel takes on the appearance of a conventional quest by a chivalric knight. Even the mode of poetry has changed, from a lively holiday scene to the solemnity of Gawain's departure. Introduced by two justly famous stanzas on the seasons (491–535), which provide a context at once natural and religious (because these are liturgical seasons) for Gawain's quest, the ceremony of Gawain's departure is narrated in highly conventional verse. We see the hero from the outside, legendary and ideal, almost saintly in these traditional set pieces: his arming, the excursus on his shield and the pentangle, and the sad farewell as he rides off, apparently to meet his death. Whereas in the opening scene Gawain himself acts with traditional, chivalric courtesy, here he is acted upon with courtly manners—he is the object of ceremony by both courtiers and narrator.

Although not much to the taste of many modern readers, the kind of conventionality found in the arming scene apparently held strong appeal for the Pearl poet's contemporary audience. (We tolerate similar kinds of conventionality and predictability, but more so in our popular prose fiction than in poetry.) The "set pieces," especially the arming of the hero, that are expected in a chivalric romance attest to its mixed heritage, since descriptions of arms are central features of epics of war and the medieval *chansons de geste*. Their absence would be a marked omission, for they lend the story significance and authority, as they idealize and exalt its hero. At the point in *Gawain* where we get these passages, there is no frivolous spirit of game and holiday merriment and almost no sense of misgiving or ironic detachment, certainly not toward the hero.

The most formal and most conventional of these descriptions surrounding Gawain's departure is the narrator's extended commentary and explication of the pentangle, which also idealizes Gawain more than any other part of the poem. Yet there are even a few aspects of the pentangle passage that potentially undercut the idealization. The pentangle is, the narrator claims, an authoritative biblical sign:

And quy þe pentangel apendez to þat prynce noble
I am in tent yow to tell, þof tary hyt me schulde.
Hit is a syngne þat Salamon set sumquyle
In bytoknyng of trawþe, bi tytle þat hit habbez.

And why the pentangel belongs to that noble prince,
I intend to tell you, even though it will delay me.
It is a sign that Solomon established one time
To betoken truth, through the title [right or name] that it has.

(623–26)

Although in this passage the narrator apparently is claiming biblical
ancestry for the pentangle, it has no such history: any development of
the pentangle as a symbol was postbiblical and largely the creation of
the poet.[25] In the context of the Pearl poet's works, poems that so frequently reproduce and evoke biblical iconography, it is particularly striking that so much importance and attention should be paid to a minor
and nonbiblical Christian symbol. The pentangle, painted on the front of
Gawain's shield, is described and analyzed at length, but the much more
orthodox iconographic image, of the Virgin Mary, on the reverse of the
shield, is mentioned quickly and never described visually.

Though the pentangle lacks the biblical ancestry claimed for it by the
narrator, it does bear Christian associations and meanings, which idealize
and moralize the values of an Arthurian knight. The five points of the
star represent five sets of fives belonging to Gawain: his five faultless
senses; his five faultless fingers (presumably standing for his actions, as
"wits" stands for his thoughts and feelings); his devotion to Christ's five
"wounds" (that is, Jesus's suffering and death) and to Mary's five joys
(like the five wounds of Christ, Mary's five joys are a subject for meditation); and finally Gawain's five virtues. These virtues (652–54) are:
"fraunchyse" (generosity, but in its broadest sense, more like "liberality"), "felaȝschyp" (fellowship, in the sense of being a loyal and loving
friend and companion), "clannes" (chastity and general purity of speech
and thought), "cortaysye" (politeness), and "pité" (compassion). Some
important Christian virtues are missing from this list of Gawain's
virtues, most notably humility. Other virtues have been altered and
adapted to chivalric values, so that they are especially appropriate to a

Christian knight. For example, the command to love one's neighbor as oneself, which is embodied in the cardinal virtue of *caritas,* is here "fellowship"—apparently love confined to one's chivalric community, not extended to one's enemies. Similarly, the virtue of liberality (also part of the larger virtue of caritas—the part we would call "charity") is a generosity that cannot function without wealth: a noble needs land and possessions in order to distribute them to others; a lord needs a fine home and servants and food in order to be a liberal host. Britton Harwood calls this virtue "obligatory largesse" and argues that in late medieval England it "became a constituent of knightly virtue."[26]

At this place in the poem there is no suggestion of any problem with the symbolism of the pentangle or with its application to Gawain. The alert reader, knowledgable about the Bible and Christian morality, might question the claims for biblical ancestry or the chivalric adaptation, and an audience well read in Arthurian romance might wonder at the virtue of chastity being applied to Gawain (since tradition praised his capacities as a lover), but at this particular point the narrator gives us no hint of these problems. The pentangle passage, like the entire arming scene, stands as an unambiguous idealization of the hero, with almost no negative note about him or even about the court and the values he represents.

The one slight negative note, the courtiers' regret that Gawain must leave on such an errand, has perhaps been made too much of by modern readers. Mostly, the court's reaction serves to verify Gawain's status, for it is primarily the kind of resigned sympathy appropriate when the good—whether saints or knights—face a heroic death. However, the courtiers' regret does indeed turn to grumbling, when they explicitly question Arthur's behavior and the values implied by it: "Who knew euer any kyng such counsel to take / As knyȝtez in cauelaciounz on Crystmasse gomnez?" (682–83; Who ever heard of a king who would follow such counsel, as comes from knights involved in disputes that are part of Christmas games?). Gawain, they say, ought rather to be given a dukedom—a kingly act, by the way, that is more common to epic than to romance. For a moment we are all made conscious of the incongruities of Gawain's situation and of similar happenings in other romances. This paragon of virtue, this embodiment of virtue, is being sent off on the stupidest of missions: a silly holiday game that will probably cost him his life.

A different kind of doubt is introduced in the account of Gawain's journey through the wilderness. In one respect, this part of the story simply evokes the tradition of the knight alone on his quest.[27] However, Gawain's actual armed conflicts are the least perilous of his adventures;

for the rapid list given of these typical fairytale and romance foes amounts to an anticlimactic dismissal:

> Sumwhyle wyth wormez he werrez and with wolues als,
> Sumwhyle wyth wodwos þat woned in þe knarrez,
> Boþe wyth bullez and berez, and borez oþerquyle.
> And etaynez þat hym anelede of þe heȝe felle.

> Sometimes he battles with serpents and with wolves also,
> Sometimes with trolls that lived in the crags,
> Both with wild bulls and bears, and boars at other times.
> And giants who chased him from the high hills.
>
> (720–23)

Greater danger than these standard perils comes from the weather, which, unlike the rather dull list of foes, is described with all the craft of the Pearl poet's art:

> For werre wrathed hym not so much þat wynter nas wors,
> When þe colde cler water fro þe cloudez schadde
> And fres er hit falle myȝt to þe fale erþe.
> Ner slayn wyth þe slete he sleped in his yrnes
> Mo nyȝtez þen innoghe, in naked rokkez
> Þeras claterande fro þe crest þe colde borne rennez
> And henged heȝe ouer his hede in hard iisseikkles.

> For battle grieved him not as much as the far worse winter,
> When the cold, clear water fell from the clouds
> And froze before it could reach the brown earth.
> Nearly dead from the sleet, he slept in his armor
> More than a few nights, among the bare rocks,
> Where the cold brook ran clattering down from the crest,
> And hung high over his head in hard icicles.
>
> (726–32)

Hardest of all his trials is Gawain's loneliness, and his lack of a refuge or shelter, even more his need for a place to attend Mass and the other holy offices of Christmas. Fighting and the hardships of the wilderness are as nothing compared to the loss of society and civilization. Although much of the romance tradition of the knight on a quest assumes his solitariness, since departure from the community is usually a necessity for a proper quest, it is unusual so to emphasize the burden of this isolation. Gawain, in fact, seems far more at home and "in his element" inside and at court (whether Arthur's or Bertilak's), feasting and playing games and engaging in ceremonial exchanges. Here again the poet has taken strongly entrenched traditions and conventions of Arthurian romance— King Arthur's court as the chivalric community and the individual knight on adventures—and used them in a way that reveals their potential incompatability.

Furthermore, by placing great importance on Gawain's problems with the cold loneliness of his quest and simultaneously belittling his deeds of battle, the poet is working against romance tradition. In most Arthurian romances, especially Chrétien's and the various Grail romances, Gawain enjoys the reputation of being the best warrior, the one whom the hero—whether Lancelot, Yvain, or Perceval—has to beat. In the Pearl poet's story this reputation survives, but as just that—a reputation and a tradition, one the courts at Camelot and Hautdesert seem to know, but not one we ever really see in action.

In some ways the Pearl poet's story thus works against tradition, even as it idealizes the hero. In one important respect the poet takes on a traditional view of Gawain and makes it explicitly an issue of the poem, namely, Gawain's reputation as a great lover. Although there is no evidence at first of this questionable reputation, and indeed Gawain's chastity is one of the five virtues symbolized in the pentangle, the inherent conflict in the traditional courtly pairing of love and honor, especially in Gawain's case, is the focus of the central action of the poem, the scenes at Hautdesert. This is the place where the poem deals directly with the values of chivalric romance. No longer set apart as an ideal, Gawain is now seen in action, confronted with his own reputation and the implications of that reputation.

Gawain's famous way with the ladies is invoked explicitly and repeatedly by all the court at Hautdesert and especially by Bertilak's Lady. After their ceremonial, almost religious, welcome of Gawain on his arrival and the traditional disarming and bathing of the knight on a quest, the Hautdesert courtiers finally learn who their guest is. They are delighted to have with them this knight, whose "mensk is þe most" (914; honor is the highest). They say:

"Now schal we semlych se sleʒtez of þewez
And þe teccheles termes of talkyng noble.
. . . .

> In menyng of manerez mere
> Þis burne now schal vus bryng.
> I hope þat may hym here
> Schal lerne of luf-talkyng."

"Now shall we nicely see the skillful craft of manners
And [hear] the perfect phrases of genteel speech.
. . . .

> Understanding of noble manners
> This knight shall now bring us.
> I believe that whoever hears him
> Shall learn about 'love-talking'."
>
> (916–17, 924–27)

This paragon, who combines honor, prowess, and virtue, is especially welcome because he will demonstrate how to speak with gentility, and in particular he will teach the court about "luf-talkyng," flirtatious but polite conversation for lovers, the kind of talk that could either precede physical lovemaking or substitute for it. Although here the only doubt in the reader's mind would be in reconciling such a reputation with the pentangle's virtue of chastity, later references, in the scenes with the Lady, are more ambivalent than this initial approving praise.

In the later passages, while the Lady herself explicitly focuses on Gawain's shortcomings as a lover, Gawain and the narrator hint that success in "luf-talkyng" would be worse than its lack. Gawain's identity and reputation make up the main subject of the reported conversation between Gawain and the Lady, particularly on the first two days. On the one hand, this is typical of romance; as Silverstein reminds us, courtly romances tend to make much of the naming of the hero (Silverstein, ed., 123, notes to lines 379–81, 401–8). For example, two of Chrétien's romances, *Yvain* and *Lancelot*, accord their respective heroes both a name and a title, the latter a kind of epithet earned through an identifying adventure: Yvain is known as "The Knight with the Lion" because he has acquired a lion as a companion while crazed and alone in the forest; and Lancelot earns the title "The Knight of the Cart" because of his notorious ride in a lowly cart while pursuing the abducted queen. On the other hand, in many romances, Wolfram von Eschenbach's *Parsifal* or Marie de France's *Milun,* for example, there are battles in which at least one knight fights in disguise, even though custom has it that opponents must first identify themselves. (This custom is implicit in *Sir Gawain and the Green Knight* in the opening scene when the Green Knight demands to know the identity of the Arthurian knight who accepts his challenge [lines 379–80].)

In certain obvious ways, then, the Lady's preoccupation with who Gawain is and whether he is really Gawain fits with this traditonal concern of romance with the hero's name and reputation. However, since the context for this preoccupation is a playful, bantering one, the traditional concern is altered and the convention even subverted. For example, on the first day that the Lady comes to Gawain's bedroom, she says she plans to keep him in bed so she can talk with him:

"For I wene wel, iwysse, Sir Wowen ʒe are,
Þat alle þe worlde worchipez; querso ʒe ride,
Your honour, your hendelayk is hendely praysed
With lordez, wyth ladyes, with alle þat lyf bere."

"For I well know, for certain, that you are Sir Gawain,
Whom all the world honors; wherever you ride,
Your honor [and] your courtesy are graciously praised
By lords, by ladies, by all who live."

(1226–29)

After beginning with this ostensibly straightforward identification of Gawain with that same knight famous for his honor and courtesy (the pairing is equivalent to Chrétien's "proesce" and "courtoisie"), the Lady immediately proceeds to a not-too-subtle invitation to lovemaking:

"And now ʒe ar here, iwysse, and we bot oure one;
My lorde and his ledez ar on lenþe faren,
Oþer burnez in her bedde, and my burdez als,
Þe dor drawen and dit with a derf haspe;

And syþen I haue in þis hous hym þat al lykez,
I schal ware my whyle wel, quyl hit lastez,
          With tale.
     ȝe ar welcum to my cors,
     Yowre awen won to wale,
     Me behouez of fyne force
     Your seruaunt be, and schale."

"And now that you are here, indeed, and we are all by ourselves—
My lord and his men have gone well away,
The other knights [are] in their beds, and my ladies also.
The door is drawn and closed with a strong clasp.
And since I have in this house the one whom all like,
I shall spend my time well, while it lasts,
          With conversation.
     You are welcome to my body,
     Your own course to choose,
     It behoves me, of strong necessity,
     To be your servant, and [so I] shall."

                                        (1230–40)

As editors point out, the statement that I have translated literally as
"You are welcome to my body," is not as blatant as it sounds in modern
English.[28] The word *cors* can be used in a more metaphorical way, referring to "person" as well as the fleshly body, especially when used in con-
junction with the personal pronoun, in this case it means "self" and "my
cors" thus translates as "me" or "myself." The Lady could be saying,
with a bit of overstatement, that she is very glad to have Gawain with
her. Nonetheless, the context, which for several lines the Lady explicitly
underscores, of a woman and a man alone in a bedroom, with the husband off on a day of hunting, definitely literalizes her concluding statement in a physical and sensual way. Even if we translate "ȝe ar welcum
to my cors" more idiomatically, as "Welcome to me and my home," it is
a fairly sexy thing for a woman to say when sitting on a man's bed while
he lies, presumably naked or scantily clothed, under the covers. Thus,
what begins as an almost formulaic, very polite, identification and praise
of a hero knight turns into a seduction ploy. The implication is that

because this knight is Gawain, the Lady wants him, and perhaps also that she can rightly expect him to want her.

Similarly, Gawain's response fits both the conventions of polite modesty and also the particular context of seduction. In words of humble self-deprecation, not unlike those in the opening scene when he confesses his unworthiness to represent Arthur's court, Gawain answers:

> "In god fayth," quoþ Gawayn, "gayn hit me þynkkez.
> Þaȝ I be not now he þat ȝe of speken—
> To reche to such reuerence as ȝe reherce here
> I am wyȝe vnworþy, I wot wel myseluen—

> "In good faith," says Gawain, "it seems to me profitable.
> Although I am not now the one you have spoken of—
> To aspire to such an honor as you have just said
> I am an unworthy creature, I myself well know—"
>
> (1241–44)

On the one hand, this could be Gawain insisting on keeping the sexual innuendoes out of their conversation and taking the Lady's invitation as a conventional, if forceful, welcome to her guest. However, I am certain the poet has Gawain knowingly respond to the implicit sexual invitation, effectively saying: "I am not the kind of knight who makes love to ladies, certainly not the famous Gawain you are hoping to seduce."

This implication is even stronger in the next stanza, in another bit of modest denial, that is at once so idiomatic and so subtle and syntactically complex that it is nearly impossible to translate (manuscript errors may add to the problem):

> "Madame," quoþ þe myry mon, "Mary yow ȝelde,
> For I haf founden, in god fayth, yowre fraunchis nobele;
> And oþer ful much of oþer folk fongen hor dedez;
> Bot þe daynté þat þay delen for my disert nys euer—
> Hit is þe worchyp of yourself, þat noȝt bot wel connez."

> "Madam," said the gay man, "May Mary reward you,
> For I have found, in good faith, your generosity to be noble;
> And some base their actions very much on those of other people;

But the honor that they give out is not of my deserving—
It is from the merit of you yourself, who knows only how to
  behave nobly."

(1263–67)

Although couched in excessively polite, almost fawning, terms, and followed by another pledge to be the Lady's servant, Gawain's denial is still
that: a denial and a refusal. Gawain is doing some very fancy, and often
quite funny, maneuvering here; his skill in fending off the Lady is equal to
that of a fine swordsman parrying an opponent's blade. Indeed, the narrator describes Gawain's behavior exactly as though he were in a fencing
match: "Þe freke ferde with defence and feted ful fayre" (1282; the war-
rrior behaved defensively and conducted himself most graciously).

The Lady's use of Gawain's reputation and identity as a weapon in her
seduction game is even stronger on the second day than on the first. She
challenges Gawain aggressively and accuses him of not being the "real
thing":

"Sir, ȝif ȝe be Wawen, wonder me þynkkez,
Wyȝe þat is so wel wrast alway to god
And connez not of compaynye þe costez vndertake."

"Sir, if you are Gawain, it's a wonder to me,
A man who is always so well disposed to good
And can understand nothing of the customs of society."
[especially in the sense of romantic relationships][29]

(1481–83)

However, Gawain continues to be equal to the Lady's aggressive moves
and correspondingly strengthens his responses. He answers that, while
greatly flattered by her attentions (1535–39), he cannot begin to teach
her about "trweluf" (1540; true love) or talk of "talez of armez" (1541;
tales of arms). For, as Gawain says to her:

"[You] þat (I wot wel) weldez more slyȝt
Of þat art, bi þe half, or a hundreth of seche
As I am, oþer euer schal in erde þer I leue,
Hit were a folé felefolde, my fre, by my trawþe."

"[You] who, as I well know, can manage more skill
In that art [of love], by twice as much, [as can] a hundred
As I am, or ever shall be, on this earth where I live,
It would be a thousandfold folly, my gracious one, by my word."

                                                    (1542–45)

Of course, this conversation is not really about Gawain or his reputation for knowledge of love and war. At the level of the story, as the characters engage in this verbal thrust-and-parry, what is going on is an
attempted, and so far successfully thwarted, seduction. Furthermore, this
seduction poses a serious threat to Gawain. By the fourth fitt (section)
we are to learn that it is not the quest to meet the Green Knight at the
Green Chapel, but the three days spent in the castle with the Lady that
constitute the real test of Gawain's integrity and honor. Even before the
Green Knight announces this, we are told that the bedroom scenes are
more than pleasant and playful flirtations. First, there is the language of
contest and combat used to describe the Lady's tactics and Gawain's
responses. Second, on the third day, when clearly Gawain is enjoying
himself more, the narrator announces that Gawain is in real danger:

Þat al watz blis and bonchef þat breke hem bitwene,
               And wynne.
      Þay lauced wordes gode,
      Much wele þen watz þerinne.
      Gret perile bitwene hem stod,
      Nif Maré of hi knyȝt mynne.

So that all was bliss and happiness that passed between them,
               And joy.
      They spoke good words,
      Much happiness then was there.
      Great peril stood between them—
      If Mary had not been mindful of her knight.

                                                    (1764–69)

The poet has made a masterful use of his stanzaic form here. The short
(two-syllable) bob summarizes the pleasure of the "luf-talkyng," and the
wheel at first continues to describe this pleasure, only to shift abruptly in

the final two lines to a totally different perspective: the moral danger in this pleasant pastime.

This new mood of seriousness continues in the following stanza:

For þat prynces of pris depresed hym so þikke,
Nurned hym so neȝe þe þred, þat nede hym bihoued
Oþer lach þer hir luf oþer lodly refuse.
He cared for his cortaysye, lest craþayn he were,
And more for his meschef ȝif he schulde make synne
And be traytor to þat tolke þat þat telde aȝt.
"God schylde!" quoþ þe schalk. "Þat schal not befalle!"

For that noble princess pressed him so heavily,
And urged him so near the limit [literally, thread], that it was
    necessary for him,
Either to receive her love or hatefully refuse it.
He cared about his courtesy, lest he be worthless,
And even more for his trouble, if he should sin
And be a traitor to that man who owned that place.
"God forbid!" said the man. "That shall not happen!"

(1770–76)

The text explains Gawain's inner turmoil with both indirect and direct discourse, one of the few times in the poem when we get something like the interior monologue so prevalent in French courtly romances (significantly, the other places where we get this in *Sir Gawain and the Green Knight* are desperate moments: when Gawain is alone in the Wirral wilderness, and when he comes upon the Green Chapel). Moreover, the language of both this stanza and the wheel immediately preceding it has changed from light innuendoes to strong and explicit words: "perile," "craþayn,"[30] "synne," and "traytor," and a direct reference to Mary. The poet has turned a happy scene of love dalliance into a heavy, moral problem.

Yet, at the same time, the third day's bedroom scene includes moments of humor, irony, and almost farce, some even funnier than those of the first two days. The most farcical of these humorous moments is also the one of most moral tension, when Gawain makes his most important and most seriously wrong move: when he accepts the Lady's "luflace." (Usually translated "girdle," a *luflace* is a kind of belt or sash that goes around a lady's tunic; the nuances of the Middle English term—literally "love belt" and thus a girdle used as a love token—are important for its use in this poem.) Just before offering her luflace, when the Lady asks Gawain for a farewell gift, he replies, certainly somewhat tongue-in-cheek, that, while he would love to give her something since she is so deserving, to give her a love token would not do. For, he says, "Hit is not your honour to haf at þis tyme / A gloue for a garysoun of Gawaynez giftez" (1806–7; It is not your privilege at this time to have for a trophy a glove from Gawain's gifts). Besides, adds Gawain, he is on a strange mission and is not carrying any luggage with love tokens to distribute (1808–10). (Just like the solitary cowboys in Hollywood westerns, this medieval hero travels light!) The Lady then makes her move, by offering to give *him* a gift: first a ring, then the luflace. At first Gawain has no trouble continuing to hold off the Lady's gifts, just as easily as he has resisted her sexual favors, but the information that the luflace could save the wearer's life is too tempting for him to ignore. Gawain's error is twofold here: first, in accepting an intimate and secret gift from his host's wife; and second, in implicitly agreeing not to tell her husband (which, of course, he could not do anyway, not without surrendering the luflace in the Exchange-of-Winnings Game).

As many readers have noted, the luflace effectively replaces the pentangle as Gawain's badge and heraldic sign, but there are important differences in the way these two signs are handled.[31] First, in contrast to his handling of the pentangle, the narrator does not tell us anything directly about the luflace—in place of authoritative and authorial information, we have only the word of the Lady (which turns out to be mostly lies) and later that of her lord (who was in on the plot), along with the conflicting views of Gawain and the court, which are articulated in the final scene at Camelot. Clearly then, the luflace is not an authoritative symbol, let alone a biblical one, as the pentangle is claimed to be. The luflace is first and foremost an article of female apparel, and its various meanings are not intrinisic, but rather attached to it by the people who use it. This is an important movement in the poem: from idealizing, authoritative Christian symbol that is purely symbol (in Augustine's terms, a *signum*), to a feminine, pseudomagical, thing (a *res*) that is an ambiguous *signum*. As Shoaf has pointed out, both of these are knots.[32] The pentangle is, as the narrator tells us, the "þe endeles knot" (630; endless knot), without beginning or end to its self-sufficient continuity.

The girdle, on the other hand, has no such fixity; it can be knotted and unknotted and passed around from wearer to wearer as easily as its meanings can be shifted. The poem's view of Gawain follows the same pattern as his signs. From the idealized Christian knight we see in the beginning, Gawain becomes a fallible human being, whose goodness is a matter of dispute.

The conflicting judgments about Gawain and his *aventure* are rendered in the last fitt of the poem, along with the different views of the luflace. The Green Knight's judgment is the most extensive and the most analytical:

> "I sende hir [my wife] to asay þe, and sothly me þynkkez
> On þe fautlest freke þat euer on fote ȝede.
> As perle bi þe quite pese is of prys more,
> So is Gawayn, in god fayth, bi oþer gay knyȝtez.
> Bot here yow lakked a lyttel, sir, and lewté yow wonted;
> Bot þat watz for no wylyde werke, ne wowyng nauþer,
> Bot for ȝe lufed your lyf—þe lasse I yow blame."

> "I sent her [my wife] to test you, and truly I think
> That you are the most faultless knight that ever walked on earth.
> As a pearl surpasses in value the white pea,
> So does Gawain, in good faith,[33] compared to other fine knights.
> But in this you were a little lacking, sir, and wanting in loyalty
> But that was for no intricate workmanship, nor for lovemaking
> either,
> But rather because you loved your life—and I blame you less."
> (2362–68)

To most readers this seems a reasonable evaluation. It is informed by a fuller knowledge of circumstances than had been available at the time of the seduction scenes, and it is spoken by the figure with the most claim to authority in the matter. Furthermore, the Green Knight's judgment is in line with orthodox Christian moral theology; *cupiditas,* whether covetousness for flesh or material things, is worse than a concern for one's own life—indeed some prudent self-protection is considered not only excusable but necessary.

On the other hand, many readers, like Gawain and the other characters in the story, tend to forget that the Green Knight is a troublesome authority figure. By his own admission, the Green Knight's games and plots have relied on magic and deceit, and they were instigated by Morgan, who learned her "craftes" (2447; magical arts) from her lover Merlin and who was motivated by a desire to scare Guenevere. All of what scholastics would see as the various kinds of causes for Gawain's adventure—how it was effected and why—are thus bad and even satanic. (In orthodox Christianity any supernatural or magical powers that are not saintly and divine must be from the devil.) Thus the Green Knight's right to judge Gawain's behavior is undercut by his associations with magic and Morgan. It is even questionable whether we should take at face value the Green Knight's disclosures about his true identity and the old woman's, but most of us do. All of these doubts, however conscious or unconscious they may be for readers, reflect an integral problem with secular fiction, and romance in particular: the lack of a trustworthy authority and the presence of magic.

However, Gawain certainly does not doubt the truth of these revelations. He only questions the Green Knight's moral judgment. Far from seeing his own behavior as nearly faultless and his worth as equal to a pearl's, Gawain condemns himself in strong language:

"For care of þy knokke, cowardyse me taȝt
To acorde me with couetyse, my kynde to forsake:
Þat is larges and lewté, þat longez to knyȝtez.
Now am I fawty and falce, and ferde haf ben euer
Of trecherye and vntrawþe—boþe bityde sorȝe
                    And care!"

"For fear of thy blow, cowardice led me
To act with covetousness, and forsake my better nature:
Which is generous and loyal, as is appropriate for knights.
Now I am sinful and without honor, I who have always feared
Treachery and dishonor—both of them bring sorrow
                    And pain!"

                                        (2379–84)

This unqualified apology, which amounts to a full confession in the Green Knight's opinion (2390–94), is not allowed to stand, but is undercut by Gawain's subsequent speech on all the women, beginning with Eve, whose wiles have brought about the downfall of their men (2414–24). This misogynist diatribe is a piece of self-justification of the worst kind. And, although we today might be more sensitive to the sexism of this kind of rationalization, a medieval audience would probably have been more aware of its weakness as moral reasoning. Shifting the blame, pointing to other sinners who have made mistakes, is to deny responsibility for one's own sins and thus to be lacking in full contrition. On the other hand, because there is a long tradition behind Gawain's speech—a tradition stretching back to the church fathers—that viewed women and female nature as the weaker side of humanity, holding men back from the higher good, it may be that the poet expected some of his audience to accept this rationalization.[34]

The respective opinions of the Green Knight and Gawain regarding Gawain's behavior are reflected in their different views of the luflace. The Green Knight offers it to Gawain as a gift, "a pure token / Of þe chaunce of þe Grene Chapel at cheualrous knyȝtez" (2398–99; a pure sign, / For chivalrous knights, of the adventure of the Green Chapel). Gawain, however, while he accepts the luflace, sees it instead as a humble reminder of his sinfulness:

"Bot your gordel," quoþ Gawayn, "—God yow forȝelde!—
Þat wyl I welde wyth guod wylle, not for þe wynne golde,
Ne þe saynt, ne þe sylk, ne þe syde pendaundes,
For wele ne for worchyp, ne for þe wlonk werkkez;
Bot in syngne of my surfet I schal se hit ofte,
When I ride in renoun, remorde to myseluen
Þe faut and þe fayntyse of þe flesche crabbed,
How tender hit is to entyse teches of fylþe.
And þus, quen pryde schal me pryk for prowes of armes,
Þe loke to þis luf-lace schal leþe my hert."

"But your girdle," said Gawain, "—May God bless you!—
That I will most willingly use, not for the lovely gold,
Nor the girdle [clasp?], nor the silk, nor the hanging pendants,
For wealth nor honor, nor for the beautiful workmanship;
But in sign of my error I shall see it often,

When I ride in fame, remember with remorse,
The faults and the frailty of the crabbed flesh,
How vulnerable it is to catching bits of dirt.
And thus, when pride shall incite me to deeds of arms,
A glance at this luflace shall humble my heart."

(2429–38)

Gawain's view of his behavior remains the same when he returns to
Camelot, where he tells of his *aventure*. Again, his sense of his error is
revealed in the terms he uses for the luflace, which he calls a "token of
vntrawþe" (2509; a token of disloyalty/dishonor/dishonesty) and "þe
bende of þis blame" (2506; the band of this fault) that he bears in his neck.

However, King Arthur and his courtiers see both Gawain and his trophy very differently—indeed with more unqualified, and almost
unthinking, admiration than even the Green Knight's positive assess-
ment. The Arthurian court's reception of Gawain and his luflace is joy-
ous and celebratory:

Þe kyng comfortez þe knyȝt, and alle þe court als
Laȝen loude þerat and luflyly acorden
Þat lordes and ledes þat longed to þe Table,
Vche burne of þe broþerhede, a bauderyk schulde haue,
A bende abelef hym aboute, of a bryȝt grene,
And þat, for sake of þat segge, in swete to were.
For þat watz acorded þe renoun of þe Rounde Table
And he honoured þat hit hade, euermore after.

The king comforts the knight, and all the court also
Laughs loudly at this and gladly agrees
That lords and knights who belong to the [Round] Table,
Each warrior of the brotherhood, a baldric should have,
A band tied about him, of bright green,
And, for the sake of that knight, to wear that, following suit.
For that [the luflace and/or the wearing of it] was granted the
    fame of the Round Table
And he who owned it would be honored for ever after.

(2513–20)

Conclusion

It is not just that King Arthur and the court see the luflace as a badge of honor and Gawain's behavior as praiseworthy. They view both from a courtly context, where laughter and game prevail, and where the values for judging a knight's behavior are chivalric values. To them Gawain has been on an *aventure,* as is proper for a knight in a romance; he has returned with a trophy, and, equally important, with a story to tell, as is essential for romance—the events of the aventure are the story of aventure and that aventure is fully betokened by the luflace. Just as Gawain has literally returned home to his chivalric community, so too the court's response of laughter and celebration returns the poem to the romance world of magic and game, a far pleasanter place than the troublesome one of moral analysis, of guilt and sin.

There is no conclusive resolution of these different contexts: the celebratory, courtly one, and the judgmental, moral one. The implication is that the two contexts cannot be reconciled. It is not just that Gawain's opinion is more negative; it belongs in the end to a world of different values. It must be remembered that, while the Green Knight's and Gawain's judgments differ, they are both argued in the language of Christian morality. When far from civilization and the chivalric community, where Gawain faces his judge alone, and where he is judged as an individual Christian, not as a representative knight of Arthur's court, the tone is serious and the language is that of moral analysis. (It is significant that when Gawain does invoke the experience of others at the Green Chapel, he does not cite knights or any characters from romance or secular history, but rather turns to biblical figures, those of sacred history.) On the one hand, this moral context is framed within the games and *aventures* of the romance world; on the other hand, the romance world is placed within the even larger contexts of British history and humanity's final home with Christ.

The poet has in this one poem shown that within that largest frame, of humanity's true place in the universe, it is possible not only to construct a playspace of romance, but to include within that playspace both sophisticated artfulness and basic moral issues. However, the very nature of romance as art and game renders it incapable of arriving at any solid conclusions about moral issues. Such conclusions can only be found in the "real" context of the world made and ruled by God, and the "tyxt of her werkkez"—the text of humanity's ultimately important deeds—can only be the Bible, never secular romance.

Epilogue

The Pearl Poet and His Poems

The Pearl poet's place in fourteenth-century English literary culture is an unusual one. Because the four poems in Cotton Nero A.x. were nearly lost and forgotten forever, remaining unread for hundreds of years after they were written (although there are some indications that for a couple of generations *Sir Gawain and the Green Knight* was known and may have inspired other Gawain tales), they necessarily stand apart from a continuing English literary tradition. Of course, the poet's dialect and verse forms no doubt made his writing almost as inaccessible to the generations living immediately after him as it is to us today. However, we need to be careful not to consider all this simply a matter of the accidents of history. I do not believe that the Pearl poet just chanced to be in a cultural milieu that happened not to survive, while the more fortunate southerners and Londoners chanced to find themselves in the dominant and surviving trend. Surely it was as apparent to the Pearl poet and his audience as it was to Chaucer, Gower, and Langland that London and its culture (including its dialect) were emerging as the center of English civilization. Furthermore, the Pearl poet's works reflect a sophistication and learning in matters both secular and spiritual that prevent us from thinking of him as a charming, but naive, poet, unaware of the world around him. Thus, there is a strong probability that the marginal position of the Pearl poet's texts, with *Sir Gawain and the Green Knight* representing only a partial exception, was as much intentional as accidental. For there is about this poet a deliberate old-fashionedness, along with what Charles Muscatine has argued is a conservative acceptance of "the orthodox forms of Christianity and of feudalism."[1]

The Pearl poet's choice of verse forms and subject matter are alike a part of this old-fashionedness. In particular, the poet's marked preference for biblical stories is one of his most consistent characteristics. Like the Wycliffite translations of the Bible into Middle English, or the sermons that narrate and comment upon Bible stories, the Pearl poet's retellings of New Testament parables and Old Testament events bring those tales into the lives of his audience. At the same time, the Pearl poet's own knowledge of the Bible and biblical iconography and exegesis renders his retellings not just accessible and relevant, but also rich in the learning of centuries of Judeo-Christian tradition.

In addition to their biblical learning, all three of the Pearl poet's explicitly religious, Christian poems contain a certain emotional and spiritual intensity of the kind imparted in the best Middle English lyrics and mystery plays. Often this spirituality is personal and even domestic and familiar, but other times, especially in *Cleanness,* there is a cold and alien quality to it, not much to modern taste. Like the Dialogues at the Foot of the Cross, found in Middle English lyrics and in some of the cycle plays, *Cleanness* evokes both the pathos of human sinners and the often harsh, but righteous and theologically orthodox, responses attributed to God. This dispassionate response is also reflected in the Pearl Maiden's flat refusal to allow the Dreamer, who is aching with desire and pleading for relief, to cross the river to her—that, she tells him, God will not allow. We moderns are naturally more drawn to views of the Creator that emphasize his love and mercy over his righteousness and justice. (That these two aspects are completely joined in divinity, rather than at odds, is part of the Pearl Maiden's lesson for the Dreamer.) However, our tastes in this regard do not separate us from the people of the Pearl poet's time. Presumably, his audience (like the poet himself) would have preferred not to think about the Creator's anger at human sinfulness— the poet explicitly remarks that to tell of that anger is a terrible burden (*Cleanness,* 4).

Sir Gawain and the Green Knight is the notable exception to the Pearl poet's preference for biblical material. For, although *Gawain* is imbued with Christian culture and morality, these are mixed in with magic, gaiety, laughter, and game in ways unusual for the Pearl poet. Even so, *Gawain* is not an exception to the poet's old-fashionedness, for it tells an old story (or what purports to be such) about legendary characters and uses a traditional verse form. Like all the other poems, *Gawain* is composed in the traditional alliterative verse that, even in the stanzaic rhymed adaptation used in *Pearl,* evokes an ancient English culture, one far from the frenchified tastes of the royal court or the bourgeois concerns of the London merchants.

All this we can only assume, inducing our impressions of the poet from the poems themselves. We know nothing more about him—not even his name. But the lack of information about his identity is consistent both with the traditional quality of his poetry and the predominately biblical nature of his subject matter. For I think it no accident that we do not know this poet's name. Two of his poems, *Patience* and *Cleanness,* are the kind of biblical retelling that in Middle English literature rarely names or describes its author. In truth, for the Middle Ages anyway, the authors of biblical retellings are ultimately God and his inspired writers, whether Moses, David, the prophets, or the New Testament evangelists, while the medieval reteller is just that—a reteller, as the Pearl poet makes clear in *Pearl,* when he keeps citing John's text. Even *Gawain,* while a courtly romance of the kind that more commonly does name its poet, evokes enough of a minstrel setting that it is not surprising that this romance offers us no identification of the poet—no Prologue like Marie's to her *Lais,* no Epilogue like Chaucer's to his *Troilus and Criseyde.* Instead, *Gawain* offers a frame of British history and culture—a kind of public source for its story, not unlike the public consciousness that is responsible for heroic poems in an oral culture. To be sure, *Gawain* is not really the kind of poem that would be produced orally by a community, nor is it even a minstrel's retelling of a popular tale; and yet the fictional context denies, in large part, its supremely individual artistry. Whenever the narrator uses the first person in *Sir Gawain and the Green Knight* (which is rare), it is with the voice of the storyteller reciting to an audience—what Nelson labels so accurately the "Listen, lordynges" pose.[2] He asks us to listen to him "a little quile"; he says he will tell us a story he heard around court or town; he wonders if the Green Knight was man or giant. Nowhere does the *Gawain* narrator assert a poet's authority over his material—the kind of insistence we get from Gottfried von Strassburg or Chrétien de Troyes, that their version is theirs, and the best one, and the final one, and nobody should dare to add to it, subtract from it, or change it in any way.

Pearl offers a similar case in a religious context. While in many ways the most personal of the four poems, and certainly the only one with the narrator as the subject, *Pearl* stops short of providing the kinds of personal details about the poet that are often found in Middle English dream visions (Chaucer's, Gower's, and, to a lesser extent, Langland's). This avoidance reflects the conflict that I believe lies at the center of *Pearl*: a conflict between the poet composing a lyrical love poem and the Christian recording a visonary experience. *Pearl* does give us a few details about the poet: that he is suffering from grief and that he has lost a beloved young girl (presumably a small daughter). But the narrator does not tell us who his patron is or what other poems he has written (facts we learn about Chaucer from *The Book of the Duchess* and from the Prologue to *The Legend of Good Women*); nor do we know if he is young or old (and past the proper age for love, as Gower says he is at the end of *Confessio Amantis*); much less are we told what this poet looks like— whether he is little and round, as we gather Chaucer is from what the Host says in *The Canterbury Tales*,[3] or long and willful (and/or named "Will"), as Langland seems to say he is in *Piers the Plowman*.[4]

The information we do get—about the poet's inner spiritual struggle—and the information we lack—about his actual identity—accord with the poem's worldview. An individual matters as a Christian soul, but not as a historical personage. Had the Pearl poet been more worldly, we would surely know more about him; probably even his name would have survived, and I suspect more manuscripts of his poems (perhaps even texts of additional poems) would have come down to us. As it is, it is integral to this poet's poetic personality that he remain anonymous. He truly fits T. S. Eliot's dictum that "a poet has not a 'personality' to express, but a particular medium";[5] and, in this case, that medium is essentially a Christian one, even when it concerns secular events, and even when it is supremely artful.

Notes and References

Chapter One

1. There are some, however, who argue that the poet had primarily a London audience for *Gawain,* an audience that would have included substantial numbers of people who came from the northwest Midlands. See Jill Mann, "Price and Value in *Sir Gawain and the Green Knight,*" *Essays in Criticism* 36 (1986): 314 and note 31; see also the historian she cites: Michael J. Bennett, "*Sir Gawain and the Green Knight* and the Literary Achievement of the North-West Midlands: The Historical Background," *Journal of Medieval History* 5 (1979): 63–88.

2. We do have evidence concerning a poet's major revisions in a few manuscripts of fourteenth-century texts. One important example is the Prologue to Chaucer's *Legend of Good Women,* which exists in two distinct versions, without any clear evidence that Chaucer meant one or the other to be the "definitive text"; see Larry D. Benson, ed., *The Riverside Chaucer* (Boston: Houghton Mifflin, 1987), 588–604; see also the explanatory notes written by M. C. E. Shaner with A. S. G. Edwards, 1060–61. Recently, however, doubt has been raised as to whether Chaucer really did write two different versions of the Prologue; see Joseph A. Dane, "The Notion of Text and Variant in the Prologue to Chaucer's *Legend of Good Women,*" *Papers of the Bibliographical Society of America* 84 (1993): 65–80. Hereafter all citations from Chaucer's works will be to the Riverside edition and will be cited parenthetically within my text.

3. For an interesting but specialized and somewhat technical discussion of these questions in regard to Old English poetry, see Douglas Moffat, "Anglo-Saxon Scribes and Old English Verse," *Speculum* 67 (1992): 805–27.

4. The omitted line is what would be line 472 of *Pearl*; the apparently jumbled lines occur toward the end of *Patience,* where what editors assume to be lines 510–12 occur a few lines later, after 513–15; the extra stanza in *Pearl* is in the fifteenth section. See Malcolm Andrew and Ronald Waldron, eds., *The Poems of the Pearl Manuscript* (Berkeley and Los Angeles: University of California Press, 1979), 76, 205, 94; hereafter cited in the text as Andrew and Waldron. Unless otherwise noted, this is the edition from which I quote.

5. J. A. Burrow, *Ricardian Poetry* (London: Routledge and Kegan Paul, 1971); hereafter cited in the text.

6. J. Huizinga, *The Waning of the Middle Ages* (New York: Doubleday, 1924), esp. 93-107.

7. Howell Chickering, Introduction in *The Study of Chivalry,* ed. Howell Chickering and Thomas H. Seiler (Kalamazoo, Mich.: Medieval Institute, 1988), 10. This very valuable, recent collection of essays on chivalry

will hereafter be cited in the text. For a discussion of chivalry particularly as it relates to *Sir Gawain and the Green Knight,* see also Wendy Clein, *Concepts of Chivalry in "Sir Gawain and the Green Knight"* (Norman: Pilgrim Press, 1987).

8.   The manuscript of *Gawain* contains the motto (or a slightly altered version of it) of the Order of the Garter, which is written in a later hand below the final lines. Some scholars have therefore argued that there is a direct connection between *Gawain* and this chivalric order, although there are real problems with making such a link. For a good summary of the varying scholarly positions on this issue, see William Vantuono, ed., *Sir Gawain and the Green Knight,* vol. 2 of *The Pearl Poems: An Omnibus Edition* (New York: Garland, 1984), 370–71; this two-volume edition will hereafter be cited as Vantuono's edition.

9.   Jean Froissart spent many years in England, under the patronage of Queen Philippa of Hainault, Edward III's wife. For readily available and translated selections from his *Chronicles,* see Froissart, *Chronicles,* ed. and trans. Geoffrey Brereton (New York: Penguin, 1968).

10.   Christine also deals, sometimes extensively, with chivalry in several of her other works; see Charity Cannon Willard, "Christine de Pizan on Chivalry," in Chickering and Seiler, *Chivalry,* 511–28. A new edition of Christine's chivalry treatise, edited and translated by Willard, is forthcoming.

11.   For a full discussion of these developments, see A. C. Partridge, *A Companion to Old and Middle English Studies* (London: André Deutsch, 1982), esp. 280–310, 353–81; for a more specialized discussion of Chancery English, see John H. Fisher, "Chancery and the Emergence of Standard Written English in the Fifteenth Century," *Speculum* 52 (1977): 870–99; and see also Fisher's recent, provocative article: "A Language Policy for Lancastrian England," *PMLA* 107 (1992): 1168–80.

12.   Derek Pearsall, *Old English and Middle English Poetry* (London: Routledge, 1977), 189–91.

13.   For a summary of the relationship of Anglo-Norman culture to native English, see J. A. Burrow, *Medieval Writers and Their Work: Middle English Literature and Its Background, 1100–1500* (Oxford: Oxford University Press, 1982), esp. 3–5.

14.   It is a matter of scholarly dispute as to how much of the Middle English alliterative poetry represented a survival (through unbroken continuity) of Anglo-Saxon traditions and how much of it was a revival (of a largely forgotten or unpracticed form). For a detailed study of Middle English alliterative poetry, which assumes that the phenomenon was primarily a revival, see Thorlac Turville-Petre, *The Alliterative Revival* (Cambridge, England: D. S. Brewer, 1977). For a good discussion of the alliterative tradition with specific reference to the Pearl poet, see A. C. Spearing, *The Gawain-Poet: A Critical Study* (Cambridge, England: Cambridge University Press, 1970), 18–32.

15.   For a valuable and sympathetic reading of these early Middle

English poems, see John M. Ganim, *Style and Consciousness in Middle English Narrative* (Princeton, N.J.: Princeton University Press, 1983), esp. 3–54.

16. Marie de France, Prologue to *Lais,* ed. Jean Rychner (Paris: Honoré Champion, 1978), line 41; for a note on the meaning of *ditiés,* see Robert Hanning and Joan Ferrante, eds. and trans., *The Lais of Marie de France* (New York: Dutton, 1978), 28, note 3. Hereafter, all citations are from Rychner's edition, and all translations from Hanning and Ferrante; both will be made in the text.

17. *Kyng Orfew (Sir Orfeo),* in Thomas C. Rumble, ed., *The Breton Lays in Middle English* (Detroit, Mich.: Wayne State University Press, 1965), 207–26.

18. Marie, in fact, includes a few Breton words throughout her lais, especially for names of characters and places; for example, she uses *"laüstic"* as the title of one of her lais, and then in the opening lines provides the French and English translations ("russignol" and "nihtegale" [nightingale], respectively; Rychner, 120).

19. See, for example, Julian of Norwich's assertion that she was a "simple unlettered creature" when she experienced her visions, in Julian of Norwich, *Showings,* ed. Edmund Colledge and James Walsh (New York: Paulist Press, 1978), 177. Colledge and Walsh argue that this means "lacking in literary skills"; see also their discussion in the Introduction, 19–20.

20. The dating of both the manuscripts and the cycle plays themselves is still debated, although the consensus is that the earliest date for any manuscript is the third quarter of the fifteenth century; see Martin Stevens, *Four Middle English Mystery Cycles* (Princeton, N.J.: Princeton University Press, 1987), 12.

21. Although the majority of these lyrics, especially from the earlier Middle English period (the thirteenth and early fourteenth centuries) are anonymous, scholarly consensus assumes a clerical author or compiler. See Rosemary Woolf, "Appendix B: Authorship," in *English Religious Lyric in the Middle Ages* (Oxford: Oxford University Press, 1968), 377–79.

22. The dialect may place only the poet, not his audience, in the northwest Midlands, according to certain scholars (see note 1 above).

23. See Marcelle Thiébaux, "Sir Gawain, the Fox Hunt, and Henry of Lancaster," *Neuphilologische Mitteilungen* 71 (1970): 469–79. In this article Thiébaux bases the connection to Lancaster on what she sees as a reference to Henry of Lancaster's *Le Livre des Seyntz Medicines* in *Sir Gawain and the Green Knight.* (Henry of Lancaster was the father of Blanche of Lancaster, the first wife of John of Gaunt.)

24. See also Chaucer's famous description of alliterative verse as "geeste 'rum, ram, ruf'" (narrate a romance by "rum, ram, ruf") in the Prologue to the Parson's Tale (X.43).

25. Burrow has taken the term from Chaucer (*Troilus and Criseyde,* 3.497) and the Pearl poet (*Gawain,* line 1009). See also Sarah Stanbury, *Seeing*

the Gawain-Poet (Philadephia: University of Pennsylvania Press, 1991), esp. 2–6.

26.   For those ready to brave the original, I recommend two things: first, read one poem at least once through in translation, choosing a favorite: probably not *Pearl,* which is the most technically crafted, nor *Cleanness,* which is hard to like; *Patience* would be a good choice because it is a short and well-paced narrative, or *Sir Gawain and the Green Knight,* of course, because it is such a wonderful and popular story, although it is the longest of the four poems; second, make use of an edition that has extensive same-page glossing or a facing-page translation, such as Vantuono's edition, or A. C. Cawley and J. J. Anderson, eds., *"Pearl," "Cleanness," "Patience," "Sir Gawain and the Green Knight"* (New York: Dutton, 1976); hereafter cited as Cawley and Anderson. The latter is probably better, since it does not provide full translations of every line and word and thus forces readers to struggle through some of the text on their own; also I, and others, have problems with a number of the comments and translations in Vantuono's edition. After this introduction, readers should be adept enough to read more of the poetry in a good, scholarly edition (Andrew and Waldron's edition still the offers the best texts of all four poems).

27.   Formulaic phrases are an unmistakable characteristic of Old English and Middle English alliterative verse, but whether these phrases are evidence of composition by oral formulaic methods has not been proved. The theory of oral formulaic composition in poetry, first developed for Homeric verse, has been applied by some scholars to early English poetry. There are clearly enough problems with fitting the theories to Anglo-Saxon verse; the difficulties greatly increase when applying them to Middle English verse, though a few scholars have tried. A good summary of the oral formulaic issue in terms of Old English poetry can be found in Pearsall, *Old English and Middle English Poetry,* 17.

28.   In The Tale of Sir Thopas, Chaucer's parody of Middle English verse romances (especially of those using the "tail rhyme" stanza), Sir Thopas is called a "doghty swayne" (VII.724)—the term, to the extent it has any particular meaning, can be translated as "bold servant."

Chapter Two

1.   See John Conley, *"Pearl* and a Lost Tradition," *Journal of English and Germanic Philology* 54 (1955): 332–47; reprinted in John Conley, ed., *The Middle English "Pearl"* (Notre Dame, Ind.: University of Notre Dame Press, 1970), 50–72; the latter collection will hereafter be cited as Conley.

2.   The Apocalypse, the last book in the New Testament, has traditionally been attributed to the Apostle John (to whom tradition also assigns the Fourth Gospel). Modern readers usually know this biblical text as the Book of Revelation, while the Middle Ages called it "the Apocalypse." The two words, *apocalypse* from the Greek and *revelation* from the Latin, have the same meaning, "an unfolding or uncovering."

3. Macrobius's text, which included The Dream of Scipio extracted from Cicero together with Macrobius's exhaustive commentary, was enormously popular in the Middle Ages—Chaucer, for example, refers to it several times—and was the only way medieval readers knew The Dream of Scipio, for they did not have Cicero's original essay that included the dream. See A. C. Spearing, *Medieval Dream Poetry* (Cambridge, England: Cambridge University Press, 1976), 8–11; and J. Stephen Russell, *The English Dream Vision: The Anatomy of a Form* (Columbus: Ohio State University Press, 1988), 58–63.

4. On the tradition of the ideal landscape, from classical literature through the Renaissance, see Ernst Robert Curtius, *European Literature of the Latin Middle Ages*, trans. Willard Trask (Princeton N.J.: Princeton University Press, 1953), 183–202.

5. Paul Piehler, *The Visionary Landscape: A Study in Medieval Allegory* (Montreal: McGill-Queen's University Press, 1971).

6. Robert O. Payne, *The Key of Remembrance* (New Haven, Conn.: Yale University Press, 1963).

7. *Pearl* also contains many features associated with love lyrics, as well as those associated with love visions; see Claude Luttrell, "An Introduction to the Dream in *Pearl*," *Medium Aevum* 47 (1978): 274–91.

8. However, there are some critics who insist that the pearl is primarily a symbol and that the poem should be read allegorically, even on the four levels of biblical allegory. See D. W. R. Robertson, "The Pearl as a Symbol," *Modern Language Notes* 65 (1950): 155–61; reprinted in Conley, 18–26. Also see Sister Mary Vincent Hillman, "Some Debatable Words in *Pearl* and Its Theme," *Modern Language Notes* 60 (1945): 241–48; reprinted in Conley, 12–17.

9. It is worth noting here, however, that there are other relationships besides father–daughter that could be closer than uncle–niece or nephew–aunt: she could be his sister, or a half-sister, or a goddaughter (who could also be a blood relative like a niece), and even, at this point anyway because we do not yet know how young she is, his mother, his wife, or his beloved.

10. "He gef" is usually translated "he gave." In fact, "gef" can be either present subjunctive or past indicative. Because in Middle English (like Latin and most Romance languages) it is not necessary to signal an optative subjunctive (a subjunctive expressing a wish or a prayer) with a word like "may," "gef" in this context can be either "he gave" or "may he give." I think it more likely that "gef" is in the subjunctive mood, since the tense of the last stanza is present or present perfect throughout (an important change from the previous stanza), while the double "amen" at the end indicates a prayer (which would call for the subjunctive mood). There is also a possibility that the verb is both past indicative and present subjunctive, thereby referring both to Christ's past salvific actions (the Crucifixion and Resurrection, as well as the Eucharist and other sacraments) and also to the Dreamer's prayer that we *will* be saved. This last kind of verbal and syntactic ambiguity is typical of the poet, who exploits the possiblities in his language for multiplying and complicating meaning.

11. Note that "hatz" gives only a "near-rhyme" with "place" and "space," and so on; even if *tz* is pronounced as a voiced consonant, close to the *s* sound of *ce,* "hatz" has a short *a* and the other *b* rhymes have a long *a.*

12. The first letter of each section is a large illuminated letter; there is also an illuminated letter at the beginning of the last stanza in section 16 (the *M* of "Motelez" [spotless] in line 961). This is presumably a scribal error, perhaps occasioned by the extra stanza in the previous section, section 15. See Sir Israel Gollancz, ed., *Facsimile Reproduction of Cotton Nero A.x. in the British Museum,* Early English Text Society, Original Series, no. 162 (London: Oxford University Press, 1923); see also the description in Vantuono's edition (xxxiv).

13. This is a different reading than most scholars give to the poem's second line, for I do not believe it to be an infinitive phrase. I punctuate the first line differently than most, placing a comma at the end, but not after "pleasaunte," so that the second line stands in apposition to the first, not as an infinitive completing "prynces paye." I believe "to clanly clos" is an adjectival phrase, describing the pearl, and that "clos" should be translated as the participial adjective "enclosed," with "to" as an intensifier, not as a signal of the infinitive.

14. See, however, Marie Borroff, "*Pearl*'s 'Maynful Mone': Crux, Simile, and Structure," in *Acts of Interpretation,* ed. Mary J. Carruthers and Elizabeth D. Kirk (Norman, Okla.: Pilgrim, 1982), 159–72; in this essay, Borroff explicates the way "mone" works in the poem.

15. Kevin Marti, "*Pearl*'s Vineyard Parable as a Textual Center," in *Body, Heart, and Text in the "Pearl"-Poet* (Lewiston, N.Y.: Edwin Mellen, 1991), 83–99.

16. See Vantuono's edition, 248, note to line 492; Vantuono translates "date" here as "beginning," while acknowledging that other editors give a meaning closer to the idea of reward.

17. See *Oxford English Dictionary,* s.v. 2, "date."

18. See P. M. Kean, *"The Pearl": An Interpretation* (London: Routledge and Kegan Paul, 1967), 175–85. Kean gives a detailed analysis of many of the link words in *Pearl,* including several I have discussed here. Although our readings are sometimes the same, her general approach is different from mine.

19. For a long time the prevailing critical view was quite otherwise: as David Aers puts it, in a footnote to an argument that parallels mine, formerly readers saw the Dreamer making a gradual progression toward an "ecstatic quest for union with God"; see "The Self Mourning: Reflections on *Pearl,*" *Speculum* 68 (1993): 67, note 50.

20. Saint Augustine, *On Christian Doctrine,* trans. D. W. R. Robertson (Indianapolis, Ind.: Bobbs-Merrill, 1958), 1.2.2., 8; hereafter cited as *Christian Doctrine* in the text.

21. As Wilson points out, this possibility was first raised by Sir Israel Gollancz in his 1891 edition of *Pearl*; see Edward Wilson, *The Gawain-Poet* (Leiden, The Netherlands: Brill, 1976), 2.

22. See also Sister Mary Vincent Hillman, *The Pearl* (Notre Dame, Ind.: University of Notre Dame Press, 1961), xix–xxi; according to Hillman, the Dreamer's "material pearl" is his soul, which the Pearl Maiden symbolizes (xx).

23. On parables as Jesus used them and as patristic exegesis allegorized them, see David M. Stanley, S.J., and Raymond E. Brown, S.S., "Aspects of New Testament Thought," in *The Jerome Biblical Commentary,* ed. Raymond E. Brown, S.S., et al. (Englewood Cliffs, N.J.: Prentice-Hall, 1968), 78: 133–34.

24. In other words, the syntax works something like this: On this mound I received the *lote* (while lying in grief for my pearl), and afterward I commended it (the *lote* and/or the pearl) to God. Note that Andrew and Waldron translate line 1207 as a relative clause using "which," obviously referring to "my pearl" as a relative pronoun: "On this mound this happened to me . . . lying prostrate for sorrow for my pearl, which I afterwards committed to God" (110, note to lines 1205–10). However, the poem has "my pearl" in a prepositional phrase and the line following as a new independent clause, with a personal pronoun ("hit"), not a relative pronoun. The effect is much looser in syntax (like the opening lines of the poem) than most translations and is therefore open to ambiguity.

Chapter Three

1. On our aesthetic judgments about "organic unity embodied in a single unified plot," see A. C. Spearing, *The Gawain-Poet,* 50.

2. Unless one counts God as the protagonist, which actually works in an interesting way; certainly the focus of much of the poem is on God's responses and actions. For a good analysis of "Divine Power" in this poem, see Spearing, *The Gawain Poet,* 65–73.

3. This is Charlotte Morse's thesis and the title of her book on *Cleanness* and *The Quest of the Holy Grail*; see Morse, *The Pattern of Judgment in the "Queste" and "Cleanness"* (Columbia: University of Missouri Press, 1978).

4. Lynn Staley Johnson, *The Voice of the Gawain-Poet* (Madison: University of Wisconsin Press, 1984), 111.

5. Although as usual I have used Andrew and Waldron for the quotation, I have made one change: adopting Vantuono's retention of the manuscript's "forering" and not emending, as many do, to "forþering." I think Vantuono is correct in translating "forering" as "fashioning" and seeing this as consistent with the poet's use of clothing imagery and symbolism in the Parable of the Wedding Feast (Vantuono's edition, 289, note to line 3). Note, also, that unlike most, I do not translate "formez" as "examples"—because I consider the term to be used in its largest sense, of rhetorical and artistic forms, which would include "examples" but also the idea of images and narrative patterns; for a more detailed discussion of this idea, see the first chapter in my book, *The Fayre Formez of the Pearl Poet* (East Lansing, Mich.: Colleagues Press, forthcoming).

6.   See Andrew and Waldron's edition, 111, note to lines 1–4.

7.   The Middle English word *make* can be translated either as "match" (that is, "equal") or "mate." Most editors translate the word here as "match," but I think it more likely to mean "mate"; or else it is a pun and means both. See Andrew and Waldron's edition, 122, note to line 248.

8.   *Drwrye* is a term used primarily for sexual love (often unlicensed sexual love); it is used as an epithet for the "luflace" the lady gives Gawain in *Gawain* (1805, 2033). See the *Middle English Dictionary,* which lists "love between God and man" as a figurative meaning for the word (the third meaning after romantic or sexual love and flirtatious behavior). However, the instances of this figurative use are few indeed (several from the Pearl poet), and it really begs the issue, since it is obvious that in each of these cases the author has deliberately chosen a word with very strongly sexual and passionate nuances in order to give force and life to the metaphor. See also Spearing, *The Gawain-Poet,* 72–73.

9.   For a fuller discussion of this important word in all the poet's works, see Derek S. Brewer, "Courtesy and the Gawain-Poet," in *Patterns of Love and Courtesy: Essays in Memory of C. S. Lewis,* ed. John Lawlor (London: Arnold, 1966), 54–85.

10.   Most editors, including Andrew and Waldron, emend the word "clene" in line 1101 to "hende" in order to make the line alliterate; here I have followed Vantuono and kept the manuscript reading.

11.   Christ's unique way of breaking the bread, barely implied in the Gospel account, eventually developed into the idea that he did it better and more cleanly than a sharp knife could—a typical medieval literalization and rationalization. See, for example, references to Christ's "clean," knifeless cutting in the N-Town play of "Christ's Appearances to the Disciples," in Peter Happé, ed., *English Mystery Plays* (New York: Penguin, 1975), 592–606, esp. 602, stanza 36. See also Morse, *Pattern of Judgment,* 181–84.

Chapter Four

1.   On Jonah as a Christ figure, see Malcolm Andrew, "Jonah and Christ," *Modern Philology* 70 (1972–1973): 230–33; and Johnson, *Voice of the "Gawain"-Poet,* 15–17.

2.   Jay Schleusner, "History and Action in *Patience,*" *PMLA* 86 (1971): 961. See also Charles Moorman, *The Pearl-Poet* (New York: Twayne, 1968), 69; Moorman likewise believes that "the poet makes very little use" of this figural interpretation of Jonah.

3.   W. A. Davenport, *The Art of the Gawain-Poet* (London: Athlone, 1978), 105–11; this study will hereafter be cited in the text. Also see Spearing, *The Gawain-Poet*; 79–90.

4.   Elizabeth Kirk, "'Who Suffreth More Than God?': Narrative Redefinition of Patience in *Patience* and *Piers Plowman,*" in *The Triumph of*

Patience, ed. Gerald J. Schiffhorst (Orlando: University Presses of Florida, 1978), 88–104.

5. Sandra Pierson Prior, "*Patience*—Beyond Apocalypse," *Modern Philology* 83 (1986): 337–48. Portions of this article are used in this chapter on *Patience.* (Copyright 1986 by the University of Chicago Press. All rights reserved. Reprinted by permission of the University of Chicago Press.)

6. In addition to serving as an important general source for apocalyptic views, 2 Peter contains a passage that has specific relevance for the poem *Cleanness*—see 2 Peter 2:4. The relevance of this biblical text for *Cleanness* was first noted by E. D. Cuffe (Ph.D. diss., University of North Carolina, 1951); see also T. D. Kelly and John T. Irwin, "The Meaning of *Cleanness*: Parable as Effective Sign," *Mediaeval Studies* 35 (1973): 244.

7. For this passage, where I think the exact wording of the Latin text is crucial for the Pearl poet, I have supplied my own, fairly literal translation of the Vulgate text; and I have included the actual Latin for the verse on the subject of God's patience.

8. Note that the Latin emphasizes the paradox by placing side by side the words "patienter" (patiently) and "agit" (he acts), the respective roots for the grammatical terms of "active and passive verbs."

9. On "the middest," see Frank Kermode, *The Sense of an Ending: Studies in the Theory of Fiction* (London: Oxford University Press, 1966), 7–8, 31, and *passim.* Kermode's study, while primarily focusing on Renaissance and modern literature, has had a great influence on my thinking about the Pearl poet's views of time, history, and narrative.

10. For an earlier and fuller discussion of this feature of *Patience,* see my article, "*Patience*—Beyond Apocalypse."

11. For other analyses, which differ in several respects and which I think are far less convincing, see F. N. M. Diekstra, "Jonah and *Patience*: The Psychology of a Prophet," *English Studies* 55 (1974): 205–17; and Johnson, *Voice of the Gawain-Poet,* 6–22.

12. On "pointing," see chapter 1.

13. See notes 1 and 2 above.

14. Christian exegetes did not actually consider most pre-Incarnation references to Christian myth to be anachronisms, since they believed the truth of Christianity to be always true and hence available to some extent to the patriarchs and prophets of the Old Testament. In religious writings, especially the cycle plays of late medieval England, figures like Noah and Abraham will, for example, invoke the Trinity. Even so, the difference in Jonah's case is that he is referring not to an eternal truth, but rather to a historical event as yet unenacted. Thus a more correct view of Jonah's reference to a crucifixion would be that it is both unintentionally anachronistic and intentionally ironic—anachronistic because in Jonah's time there were as yet no Romans and therefore no execution by crucifixion (a peculiarly Roman invention)—but this the Pearl poet probably did not know; and ironic since Jonah grimly imagines a particular form of per-

secution the Ninevites would be sure to inflict upon him, without however knowing, as we and the poet do, that this was to be the very torture God's incarnate son would undergo.

15. In the manuscript illustration for this scene in *Patience,* the artist shows Jonah being swallowed by the whale while the sailors are still holding onto his feet, a motif found in some biblical illustrations of this episode. See Gollancz, *Facsimile Reproduction of Cotton Nero A.x.,* fol. 86b; reproduced in Vantuono's edition, vol. 2.

16. See Johnson, *Voice of the Gawain-Poet,* 11, for a very different reading of the effect of this addition by the Pearl poet. Essentially, Johnson states that "this is not a prayer of repentance but a bargain," which reveals "Jonah's lack of spiritual renewal." Davenport, however, believes that the poet has added the first prayer "probably to justify the logic of the Vulgate's past tense *Clamavi*" (*Art of the Gawain-Poet,* 122). See also Edward Wilson, *The Gawain-Poet,* 65; Wilson says that the first prayer makes thanksgiving "logically plausible."

17. Another way to read this phrase is as a reference to Jonah's body, especially as part of a metaphorical reading of the entire passage: Jonah as suffering man, enclosed in his earthly flesh and surrounded by tribulation and pain, and awaiting release from both the flesh and the pain. Under the circumstances, I believe the poet's addition of the reference to the body is meant to render Jonah's prayer more literal and more directly relevant to Jonah's situation, since if a metaphorical reading were sought, there would be less reason to make changes to the biblical text. However, it is possible the poet would have been aware (and hoped his audience was too) that his addition made Jonah's situation at once more literal and specific and also more figural and tropological.

18. Exegetes connected the Jonah psalm with Psalm 68/69, "Salvum me" (Save me), with which it has close verbal parallels, and they believed Psalm 68/69 prefigured the Crucifixion. Jerome, for example, says that Psalm 68 describes "the passion of Christ" (*Patrologiae Cursus Completus* . . . Series Latina, ed. J. P. Migne [Paris, 1878–90], 25, column 1189; translation mine). Hereafter *Patrologiae* will be cited parenthetically in the text. Illustrations in late medieval psalters, however, usually point to the general human, rather than to a specifically Christological reading, for they often depict a man in the curve of the *S* (the initial letter of "Salve"), literally drowning in the depths, with his hands raised in prayer—he is clearly not Christ, for there is no nimbus.

19. Most scholars assume that "nos" in this line means literally "nose" in Modern English, which is used metaphorically here. However, the *Middle English Dictionary* gives "opening" as one meaning for Middle English *nose* (citing, of course, this line). Since we do not have any other attested usage, I see no reason to take away the poet's own striking metaphor by reducing it to a simple gloss. See Vantuono's edition, 229, note to line 451.

20. This is different from what Kermode sees as the usual tendency caused by humanity's "deep need for 'intelligible Ends.'" According to

Kermode, "We project ourselves—a small, humble elect, perhaps, past the End, so as to see the structure whole, a thing we cannot do from our spot of time in the middle" (*Sense of an Ending,* 8).

21.   Other editors have the narrator's voice pick up right after God stops speaking, wherever they indicate that occurs. I think Andrew and Waldron have clearly made the right choice about the respective voices, though I do not agree with them that the narrator's voice is "in the *persona* of a preacher" (italics theirs). The narrator of *Patience* has become a prophet, although a prophet in the post-Incarnation world of fourteenth-century England.

22.   See, for example, Isaiah 7:7, when the Lord sends Isaiah to meet Ahaz. There are, of course, many variations on the formula; what is important to note is that the Lord speaks directly (usually in the first person) through the mouth of His prophet.

Chapter Five

1.   For readers who wish a more comprehensive introduction to the poem and its criticism, there are, in addition to the general bibliographies on the poet, bibliographies specific to this poem: Morton W. Bloomfield, "*Sir Gawain and the Green Knight*: An Appraisal," *PMLA* 76 (1961): 7–19; reprinted in *Critical Studies of "Sir Gawain and the Green Knight,"* ed. Donald R. Howard and Christian Zacher (Notre Dame, Ind.: University of Notre Dame Press, 1968), 24–55; this collection will hereafter be cited as Howard and Zacher. Also see Robert J. Blanch, *"Sir Gawain and the Green Knight": A Reference Guide* (Troy, N.Y.: Whitston, 1983).

2.   Charles Muscatine, *Poetry and Crisis in the Age of Chaucer* (Notre Dame, Ind.: University of Notre Dame Press, 1972), 69.

3.   Sheila Fisher, "Leaving Morgan Aside: Women, History, and Revisionism in *Sir Gawain and the Green Knight,"* in *The Passing of Arthur: New Essays in Arthurian Tradition,* ed. Christopher Baswell and William Sharpe (New York: Garland, 1988), 129–51; this collection will hereafter be cited as Baswell and Sharpe.

4.   R. A. Shoaf, *The Poem as Green Girdle: Commercium in "Sir Gawain and the Green Knight"* (Gainesville: University of Florida Press, 1984). See also Jill Mann, "Price and Value in *Sir Gawain and the Green Knight,"* *Essays in Criticism* 36 (1986): 294–318. Hereafter both studies will be cited in the text.

5.   For a discussion of chivalry in terms of chivalric romance, see Robert W. Hanning, "The Criticism of Chivalric Epic and Romance," in Chickering and Seiler, eds., *The Study of Chivalry,* 91–113. For more information, see some of the other articles in this collection and also Maurice Keen, *Chivalry* (New Haven, Conn.: Yale University Press, 1984).

6.   The pairing of *proesce* and *courtoisie* occurs often in Chrétien de Troyes's romances. See, for example, the passage in which a lady and her moth-

er are said to have heard many times of Yvain's "cortoisie" and "grant proesce": *The Knight with the Lion, or Yvain (Le Chevalier au Lion)*, ed. and trans. William W. Kibler (New York: Garland, 1985), lines 4024–25.

7.   See *Middle English Dictionary*, s.v., *leik*, n.

8.   See Burrow's discussion of this passage, in which he points out the "touch of bookishness" in the Lady's speech, in *A Reading of "Sir Gawain and the Green Knight"* (New York: Barnes and Noble, 1966), 92; this study will hereafter be cited in my text.

9.   See Northrop Frye, *The Secular Scripture: A Study of the Structure of Romance* (Cambridge, Mass.: Harvard University Press, 1976), esp. 3–31, for a different view of romance, one which sees it primarily as a popular literary form, which lacks the authority of myth. Frye makes it clear that he is not talking primarily about medieval romance (4). However, to the extent that Frye's generic principles hold true for medieval romance, we could look upon the use of historical and legendary figures in chivalric romance as the particular community's way of absorbing the romance tale into its authoritative mythology——what Frye calls "mythical imperialism" (13).

10.   Robert W. Hanning, *The Vision of History in Early Britain* (New York: Columbia Univeristy Press, 1966), 122.

11.   According to Susan Crane, this concern to distinguish English romances and their romance heroes from those on the Continent began in the twelfth century and can be found in Anglo-Norman romances; see her *Insular Romance: Politics, Faith, and Culture in Anglo-Norman and Middle English Literature* (Berkeley and Los Angeles: University of California Press, 1986), esp. 216; hereafter this study will be cited in the text.

12.   For a summary of Gawain's place in medieval Arthurian literature, see the entry on him in *The Arthurian Encyclopedia*, ed. Norris J. Lacy (New York: Garland, 1986), 206–8.

13.   Charles Dunn, "Romances Derived from English Legends," in *A Manual of the Writings in Middle English*, ed. J. Burke Severs, vol. 1, *Romances* (New Haven, Conn.: Connecticut Academy of Arts and Sciences, 1967), 25–31. For a collection of translated versions of some of these romances, see *Richard the Lion-Hearted and Other Medieval English Romances*, trans. and ed. Bradford B. Broughton (New York: Dutton, 1966).

14.   As Crane puts it, "For the early insular poets Old French *courtoisie* is alien and implausible, but later poets embrace it as a source of heroic value by rejecting its claims to exclusivity and high refinement" (221).

15.   John Ganim, *Style and Consciousness in Middle English Narrative*, 17–18. See also Burrow, *Medieval Writers and Their Work*, 51–52.

16.   See Burrow, *Ricardian Poetry*, 13. For another good discussion of this sense of orality, see William Nelson, "From 'Listen Lordings' to 'Dear Reader,'" *University of Toronto Quarterly* 46 (1976–77): 110–224.

17.   For a slightly different reading of the opening, see Larry D. Benson,

Art and Tradition in "Sir Gawain and the Green Knight" (New Brunswick, N.J.: Rutgers Unversity Press, 1965), 96–97.

18.   Theodore Silverstein, ed., *Sir Gawain and the Green Knight* (Chicago: University of Chicago Press, 1984, 113, note to lines 8, 11, 12; this edition is hereafter cited in my text as Silverstein's edition. See also Silverstein, "Sir Gawain, Dear Brutus and Britain's Fortunate Founding: A Study of Comedy and Convention," *Modern Philology* 62 (1965): 189–206.

19.   For a discussion of what a "lay" might be, see Rumble, ed., *Breton Lays in Middle English,* xiii–xv; see also my discussion of the Breton lays in chapter 1.

20.   *Childgered* is not a compound found in any other text—whether one translates it as "boyish/youthful" or in a more negative way, as "childish," depends upon how morally one reads both this passage and the whole poem. While I think ultimately the poet is questioning the ideals and practices of chivalry and romance, I do not believe that here he is deliberately sneaking in a moralizing remark—it would be too heavyhanded, and even snide, in a passage that is otherwise gay and playful and celebratory in its tone. See Andrew and Waldron's edition, 210, note to lines 86–89; compare Vantuono's edition, 2:244–45, notes to lines 85–106 and 86.

21.   See Silverstein's note on this in his edition of the poem, 117–18, note to lines 90–102.

22.   Frederick B. Jonassen, "Elements from the Traditional Drama of England in *Sir Gawain and the Green Knight,*" *Viator* 17 (1986): 237. As the title of his article indicates, Jonassen argues that the drama (both the Mummers' Play and certain cycle plays) provided an important influence and source for this holiday mixture of gaiety and seriousness.

23.   Still the best discussion of this important aspect of the poem is Donald R. Howard, "Structure and Symmetry in *Sir Gawain,*" *Speculum* 39 (1964): 425–33; reprinted in Howard and Zacher, 159–73.

24.   On the privileged relationship between maternal uncle and nephew, see Marc Bloch, *Feudal Society,* 2 vols. trans. L. A. Manyon (Chicago: University of Chicago Press, 1964), 1:137; and Georges Duby, *The Chivalrous Society,* trans. Cynthia Postan (Berkeley and Los Angeles: University of California Press, 1977), 141.

25.   For more on the pentangle, which had a full history in the Middle Ages, although as the "Seal of Solomon," not as a "pentangle," see Silverstein's edition, 129–31; and Andrew and Waldron's edition, 230–33, all notes to relevant lines and terms. As far as I know, no one comments on the irony involved in this most biblical of poets citing a biblical authority (Solomon) for a symbol that is nowhere in the Bible.

26.   Britton Harwood, *"Gawain* and the Gift," *PMLA* 106 (1991): 485.

27.   On the centrality of the quest for *aventure,* see Erich Auerbach, "The Knight Sets Forth," in *Mimesis,* trans. Willard R. Trask (Princeton, N.J.:

Princeton University Press, 1953), 123–42, esp. 136; on the solitariness of the
quest, see R. W. Southern, "From Epic to Romance," in *The Making of the
Middle Ages* (New Haven, Conn.: Yale University Press, 1953), 219–57, esp.
244–45.

28.   See, for example, Andrew and Waldron's edition, 253, note to
1237f; see also Burrow, *A Reading of "Sir Gawain,"* 80–81.

29.   As Andrew and Waldron put it, "*{C}ompaynye* already has some of
the amorous connotation of the modern 'keep company' as it also has in
Chaucer's lines on the Wife of Bath" (262, note to 1483; compare the General
Prologue of the *Canterbury Tales,* lines 460–61).

30.   The word *craypayn* is a matter of some dispute—see Silverstein's
edition, 157–59, note to line 1773.

31.   On the pentangle and medieval sign theory, see Burrow, *A Reading
of "Sir Gawain,"* 187–89. Two recent discussions of the luflace and the pentangle as signs are R. A. Shoaf, "The 'Syngne of Surfet' and the Surfeit of Signs," in
Baswell and Sharpe, 160–65; and Geraldine Heng, "Feminine Knots and the
Other *Sir Gawain and the Green Knight,*" *PMLA* 106 (1991): 500–14. Of these
two, I find Shoaf's discussion far more valuable.

32.   Shoaf, *The Poem as Green Girdle,* 75; see also his "The 'Signe of
Surfet,'" 160.

33.   Probably "in good faith" is here used simply as an intensifying aside
(equivalent to "truly"), but Andrew and Waldron make the plausible suggestion that the phrase might literally mean "in respect of good faith"—and thus
be an explanatory reference to Gawain's integrity (see Andrew and Waldron's
edition, 293, note to line 2365).

34.   Ganim has an unusual and interesting reading of this speech; see
Style and Consciousness in Middle English Narrative, 69.

Epilogue

1.   Muscatine, *Poetry and Crisis in the Age of Chaucer,* 37.
2.   Nelson, "From 'Listen Lordings' to 'Dear Reader,'" 110–224.
3.   *The Canterbury Tales,* VII.700–702.
4.   For the several passages in the various texts of *Piers the Plowman* that
are likely to be punning references to Langland's name and physical appearance,
see the Introduction in *Piers the Plowman: A Critical Edition of the A Version,* ed.
Thomas A. Knott and David Fowler (Baltimore, Md.: Johns Hopkins
University Press, 1952), 8–11.
5.   T. S. Eliot, "Tradition and the Individual Talent," in *The Sacred
Wood* (New York: Barnes and Noble, 1960), 47–59.

Selected Bibliography

The following is a briefly annotated bibliography, which is intended to introduce readers to the poet and his background. I have made it quite selective and aimed it at the new reader because enough Pearl poet bibliographies exist for specialists and advanced researchers. My selection is affected by my own critical and scholarly biases, although I have tried to be as fair as possible—if not always impartial, at least honest about my partiality. I have grouped the entries under four headings: Editions and Translations; Bibliography and Reference; Background; and Critical Studies—this last subdivided into a general list of studies involving more than one poem and separate lists for studies specific to each poem. These separate lists are vastly different in length, owing to the great differences in critical attention paid to their respective poems. In fact, the list of critical studies focusing on *Cleanness,* while very short, is proportionately more inclusive than those for *Pearl* or *Sir Gawain and the Green Knight.* Studies of general issues, like genre, that include specific chapters or sections on one of the poems have been included only under "Background," with a note about the specific poem(s) discussed—I have otherwise made no attempt to cross-reference. Under the heading "Editions and Translations" I have not listed all available editions, but only the few that I think best, in terms of quality, availability, cost, and accessibility, particularly for the nonspecialist.

Editions and Translations

Anderson, J. J., ed. *Cleanness.* New York: Barnes and Noble, 1977.
————, ed. *Patience.* New York: Barnes and Noble, 1969.
Anderson, J. J., and A. C. Cawley, eds. *"Pearl," "Cleanness," "Patience," "Sir Gawain and the Green Knight."* New York: Dutton, 1962, 1976. A one-volume edition of all four poems, including the two edited separately by Anderson, plus *Pearl* and *Gawain,* which are also published as a pair under one cover. These editions feature same-page glossing, with all difficult lines translated in full at the bottom of the page. The editions also have the advantage, especially for new readers, of being inexpensive (although this bargain results in a book that falls apart fairly quickly).
Andrew, Malcolm, and Ronald Waldron, eds. *The Poems of the Pearl Manuscript: "Pearl," "Cleanness," "Patience," "Sir Gawain and the Green Knight."* Berkeley and Los Angeles: University of California Press,

1979. Overall, the best of the editions containing all four poems. Scholarly enough for the most experienced readers, but good too for any new readers ready to try the original; not outrageously expensive and available in paperback.

Borroff, Marie, trans. *Pearl.* New York: Norton, 1977. An inexpensive, paperback, verse translation, although many have trouble with some of the renderings—inevitably, given the nature of the poem's language and versification.

———, trans. *Sir Gawain and the Green Knight.* New York: Norton, 1967. Probably the most readily available and widely anthologized of the verse translations of this poem.

Gordon, E. V. *Pearl.* Oxford: Clarendon Press, 1953. A sound, scholarly edition. Not intended for the reader who needs much help with the language, since it lacks same-page glossing; moreover, the critical commentary is somewhat dated. Still I like it much better than the edition, with facing-page translation, by M. V. Hillman, whose highly allegorical and theological reading of the poem has unduly affected her translation.

Silverstein, Theodore. *"Sir Gawain and the Green Knight": A New Critical Edition.* Chicago: University of Chicago Press, 1984. My favorite of the recent single-gle editions of this poem—useful for a wide range of readers.

Bibliography and Reference

Andrew, Malcolm. *The Gawain-Poet: An Annotated Bibliography, 1839–1977.* New York: Garland, 1979. A very useful bibliography, which was supplemented by a 1989 article by Michael Foley (listed below).

Bloomfield, Morton. *"Sir Gawain and the Green Knight:* An Appraisal." *PMLA* 76 (1961): 7–19; reprinted in *Critical Studies of "Sir Gawain and the Green Knight,"* edited by Donald R. Howard and Christian Zacher, 24–55. Notre Dame, Ind.: University of Notre Dame Press, 1968. The latter collection will be cited hereafter as Howard and Zacher. Although somewhat discursive and offering critical insights, this article is primarily a bibiographical essay covering scholarly and critical work on the poem through the 1950s.

Foley, Michael. "The Gawain-Poet: An Annotated Bibliography, 1978–1985." *Chaucer Review* 23 (1989): 251–82. The most recent published bibiography on the poet, supplementing the previous ones. For bibliography since 1985, readers should consult the *MLA Bibliography,* published annually in book form and on line at many research libraries.

Gollancz, Sir Israel, ed. *Facsimile Reproduction of Cotton Nero A.x. in the British Museum.* Early English Text Society, Original Series, no. 162. London: Oxford University Press, 1923. Self-explanatory. Those not able to decipher the difficult Gothic script can still enjoy the reproductions of the illuminations.

Kottler, Barnet, and Alan M. Markman. *A Concordance to Five Middle English Poems.* Pittsburgh, Pa.: University of Pittsburgh Press, 1966. "Five" poems because the compliers have included *St. Erkenwald,* which some scholars, especially earlier ones, believe to be written by the Pearl poet. This concordance is a very useful tool for those working closely with the poet's language.

Middle English Dictionary. Edited by Hans Kurath et al. Ann Arbor: University of Michigan Press, 1952–.

Background in Language, Literature, and History

Augustine, Saint. *On Christian Doctrine.* Translated by D. W. R. Robertson. Indianapolis, Ind.: Bobbs-Merrill, 1958. Even for those of us who resist overly exegetical readings, this treatise is almost essential for reading medieval literature; for the Pearl poet, Augustine's discussion of *signa* (signs) and *res* (things) is especially useful.

Baswell, Christopher, and William Sharpe, eds. *The Passing of Arthur: New Essays in Arthurian Tradition.* Garland Reference Library of Humanities, no. 78. New York: Garland, 1988. Useful both as background on Arthurian tradition and for its essays specifically on *Sir Gawain and the Green Knight.* Hereafter cited as Baswell and Sharpe.

Benson, Larry D. "The Literary Character of Anglo-Saxon Formulaic Poetry." *PMLA* 81 (1966): 334–41. Although specifically about Old English poetry, this is an intelligent discussion of the issue of formulaic verse and its relationship to both oral and literate cultures.

Burrow, John A. *Medieval Writers and Their Work: Middle English Literature and Its Background, 1100–1500.* New York: Oxford University Press, 1982. A useful and intelligent introduction to the period and its literature, which offers new insights both for newcomers and the more experienced.

———. *Ricardian Poetry: Chaucer, Gower, Langland and the "Gawain" Poet.* London: Routledge and Kegan Paul, 1971. A study of the poetry of the Pearl poet's time, with a focus on common features. Readable, learned, and insightful.

Carruthers, Mary J., and Elizabeth D. Kirk. *Acts of Interpretation: The Text in Its Contexts.* Norman, Okla.: Pilgrim, 1982. Hereafter cited as Carruthers and Kirk, this collection, in honor of E. Talbot Donaldson, includes two essays on the Pearl poet's works—one on *Pearl* and one on *Gawain* (both listed below)—as well as other studies, which though somewhat specialized provide a valuable and sophisticated context for reading the Pearl poet.

Chickering, Howell, and Thomas H. Seiler, eds. *The Study of Chivalry.* Kalamazoo, Mich.: Medieval Institute Publications, 1988. Many of the articles are probably too specialized for the new reader of romance, but the Introduction and Hanning's essay (listed below) are useful as background. In general, Keen's study of chivalry is more comprehensive, but this one is more provocative and up to date.

Crane, Susan. *Insular Romance: Politics, Faith, and Culture in Anglo-Norman and Middle English Literature.* Berkeley and Los Angeles: University of California Press, 1986. A detailed discussion of the romance genre in medieval England. Crane argues that "Anglo-Norman romances and their Middle English versions form a distinctively 'insular' body of works" (1).

Frye, Northrop. *The Secular Scripture: A Study of the Structure of Romance.* Cambridge, Mass.: Harvard University Press, 1976. Although primarily a study of prose romance (mostly post-Renaissance), this is still a work that raises some interesting issues about the genre of romance.

Ganim, John. *Style and Consciousness in Middle English Narrative.* Princeton, N.J.: Princeton University Press, 1983. An intelligent and useful study, good both as general background and also for its specific chapter on *Gawain.*

Keen, Maurice. *Chivalry.* New Haven, Conn.: Yale University Press, 1984. A comprehensive recent study of chivalry, perhaps better used as a reference for new students, but there is much of interest in this book.

Lacy, Norris J., ed. *The Arthurian Encyclopedia.* New York: Garland, 1986. Just what it says it is: an encyclopedia filled with Arthurian lore, written by historians, art historians, and literary scholars. Useful not only for its specific articles on the figure of Gawain and the Pearl poet's romance, but also as a reference tool for the Arthurian traditions at work in the poem.

Muscatine, Charles. *Poetry and Crisis in the Age of Chaucer.* Notre Dame, Ind.: University of Notre Dame Press, 1972. A small and provocative book on the major poets of the late fourteenth century. The chapter on the Pearl poet, entitled "The Pearl Poet: Style as Defense," is a thoughtful introduction for new readers, who could also profit from the chapters on Chaucer and Langland, as well as the first chapter, "Relevance, Poetic Style, and Cultural Crisis: An Introduction."

Nolan, Barbara. *The Gothic Visionary Perspective.* Princeton, N.J.: Princeton University Press, 1977. Good as background on the dream vision genre and the artistic, exegetical, and literary traditions behind it, as well as for its chapter devoted to *Pearl.*

Partridge, A. C. *A Companion to Old and Middle English Studies.* London: André Deutsch, 1982; Totowa, N.J.: Barnes and Noble, 1982. Lengthy background in history and language for students of both Old and Middle English literature; probably too detailed for the new reader, but its scholarly and comprehensive approach makes it an outstanding reference work.

Pearsall, Derek. *Old English and Middle English Poetry.* Routledge History of English Poetry, vol. 1. London: Routledge and Kegan Paul, 1977. In size, coverage, and detail, this text ranks in the middle of the three background studies of medieval English literature (the others are Partridge's

Companion and Burrow's *Medieval Writers*); with a special section on the Pearl poet and *Gawain* in his chapter on "Alliterative Poetry."

Piehler, Paul. *The Visionary Landscape: A Study in Medieval Allegory.* Montreal: McGill-Queen's University Press, 1971. An interesting study of medieval dream poetry, drawing on Jungian principles, with a chapter on *Pearl.*

Russell, J. Stephen. *The English Dream Vision: Anatomy of a Form.* Columbus: Ohio State University Press, 1988. A recent study of the dream vision genre, reflecting some of the latest critical approaches and theories, with a 15-page section on *"Pearl* and the Discourse of Eschatology."

Salter, Elizabeth. *Fourteenth-Century English Poetry: Contexts and Readings.* Oxford: Clarendon Press, 1983. A good discussion of the distinctive features of poetry in an age when Salter says "it was a universal medium," both "high art and doggerel" (1).

Spearing, Anthony C. *Medieval Dream Poetry.* Cambridge, England: Cambridge University Press, 1976. Intelligent and still useful; the best introduction to this important medieval genre, with a good chapter on dream poems in the alliterative tradition, including *Pearl.*

Thiébaux, Marcelle. "The Mediaeval Chase." *Speculum* 42 (1967): 260–74. Excellent background on the hunt; Thiébaux also wrote a book-length study of the hunt in medieval literature, but this article is perhaps the best place for the interested reader to begin.

Turville-Petre, Thorlac. *The Alliterative Revival.* Totowa, N.J.: Rowman and Littlefield, 1977. A book-length study of alliterative poetry in Middle English, based on the assumption that this poetry represents primarily a revival, rather than a continuation, of Old English verse forms.

Waldron, Ronald A. "Oral-Formulaic Technique and Middle English Alliterative Poetry." *Speculum* 32 (1957): 792–804. An attempt to apply oral-formulaic theories to Middle English alliterative poetry—for me an unsuccesful, unconvincing attempt.

CRITICAL STUDIES
General

Brewer, Derek S. "Courtesy and the Gawain-Poet." In *Patterns of Love and Courtesy: Essays in Memory of C. S. Lewis,* edited by John Lawlor, 54–85. London: Arnold, 1966. One of the earliest analyses that works with a feature common to all four poems—in this case the important term and concept of "courtesy."

Davenport, W. A. *The Art of the Gawain-Poet.* London: Athlone, 1978. A detailed close reading of each poem and its "art"; the art Davenport is most interested in is the poet's complexity within unity and his "search for ironic expression" (215).

Hieatt, A. Kent. "Symbolic and Narrative Patterns in *Pearl, Cleanness, Patience,*
    and *Gawain.*" *English Studies in Canada* 2 (1976): 125–43. A good study
    of the Pearl poet's poetic and narrative structures and their meaning.
Johnson, Lynn Staley. *The Voice of the Gawain-Poet.* Madison: University of
    Wisconsin Press, 1984. Although the title suggests that this full-length
    study might concern poetic style or rhetoric, Johnson in fact gives a par-
    tially updated, but essentially Robertsonian reading of the poet's works in
    light of Augustinian views of interpretation.
Moorman, Charles. *The Pearl-Poet.* New York: Twayne, 1968. The original
    monograph in the Twayne English Authors series and useful for its reflec-
    tion of earlier critical views, especially those I have not much used.
Spearing, A. C. *The Gawain-Poet.* Cambridge, England: Cambridge University
    Press, 1970. Probably the best of the four monographs on the poet pub-
    lished in the 1970s—certainly the best introduction for the new reader.
    Primarily a close reading of each poem separately, but with some discus-
    sion of common motifs and concerns, including "Divine Power" in
    Cleanness and *Patience* and the poet's ironically humorous views of human
    characters.
Stanbury, Sarah. *Seeing the "Gawain"-Poet.* Philadephia: University of
    Pennsylvania Press, 1991. A recent, full-length study of all four poems,
    in which the focus is on the poet's famous descriptive technique through
    "ocular reception," what Burrow (*Ricardian Poetry,* 69–75) calls "point-
    ing" and Stanbury considers a "visual hermeneutic" (5).
Vantuono, William. "*Patience, Cleanness, Pearl,* and *Gawain*: The Case for
    Common Authorship." *Annuale Medievale* 12 (1971): 37–69. A thor-
    ough, although sometimes a bit flat-footed, discussion of the issue of
    authorship for the poems of Cotton Nero A.x.
Wilson, Edward. *The Gawain-Poet.* Leiden, The Netherlands: Brill, 1976. Both
    sensible and scholarly, with much attention paid to biblical and secular
    sources. Wilson has chosen "to concentrate on what is of unique literary
    significance in each poem" rather than to look for common "patterns of
    thought or poetic method" (xi).

Pearl

Aers, David. "The Self Mourning: Reflections on *Pearl,*" *Speculum* 68 (1993):
    54–73. A very recent and intelligent article that sides with those who
    believe *Pearl* is a record of loss and grief, not a consolation.
Bishop, Ian. *"Pearl" in Its Setting.* New York: Barnes and Noble, 1968. A criti-
    cal study that concentrates on the sources and other background materi-
    als for the poem in an attempt to explain its allegory. Not a study I find
    helpful, but a good representative of a different approach from mine.
Bogdanos, Theodore. *"Pearl": Image of the Ineffable.* University Park:
    Pennsylvania State University Press, 1983. A monograph offering a

lengthy study of *Pearl*'s "symbolic development" (1), which Bogdanos believes is grounded "in the medieval notion of analogy" (5).

Borroff, Marie. *"Pearl's* 'Maynful Mone': Crux, Simile, and Structure."* In Carruthers and Kirk, 159–72. An insightful study, through close stylistic and textual analysis, of one of the poem's more elusive images.

Conley, John, ed. *The Middle English "Pearl": Critical Essays.* Notre Dame, Ind.: University of Notre Dame Press, 1970. Hereafter cited as Conley. A collection of critical essays on *Pearl* (all reprints), most from the 1950s and 1960s; a good representation of the varied critical approaches of that time.

———. *"Pearl* and a Lost Tradition." *Journal of English and Germanic Philology* 54 (1955): 332–47. Reprinted in Conley, 50–72. In addition to making its own argument for the genre of *Pearl* as a consolation, this article summarizes and gives a bibliography for the other positions.

Hamilton, Marie Padgett. "The Meaning of the Middle English *Pearl.*" *PMLA* 70 (1955): 805–24. Reprinted in *Middle English Survey,* edited by Edward Vasta, 117–45. Notre Dame, Ind.: University of Notre Dame Press, 1965. The latter collection will hereafter be cited as Vasta. An essay in which Hamilton offers a "solution to the mystery of *Pearl*"—a solution I find even more unconvincing than the "mystery" it purports to solve.

Johnson, Wendell Stacey. "The Imagery and Diction of *The Pearl*: Toward an Interpretation." *ELH* 20 (1953): 161–80. Reprinted in Vasta, 93–115. Reprinted also in Conley, 93–115. Primarily a new critical analysis of the poem's language and imagery.

Kean, P. M. *"The Pearl": An Interpretation.* London: Routledge and Kegan Paul, 1967. An exhaustive and detailed analysis of *Pearl,* with particular attention to language, imagery, and sources. Probably more useful in parts than as a whole, especially for the new reader.

Luttrell, Claude. "An Introduction to the Dream in *Pearl.*" *Medium Aevum* 47 (1978): 274–91. An important essay that focuses on the language of love in the opening stanzas, although the conclusions Luttrell draws are different from mine.

Macrae-Gibson, O. D. *"Pearl*: The Link-Words and the Thematic Structure." *Neophilologus* 52 (1968): 54–64. Reprinted in Conley, 203–19. Focuses, as the title indicates, on the thematic role of the link-words and their meaning, while deemphasizing their function as language play.

Marti, Kevin. *Body, Heart, and Text in the "Pearl"-Poet.* Lewiston, N.Y.: Mellen, 1991. A highly theoretical study taking advantage of the current fashionable interest in the body, especially as a literary space.

Moorman, Charles. "The Role of the Narrator in *Pearl.*" *Modern Philology* 53 (1955): 73–81. Reprinted in Conley, 103–21. An analysis of the development of the narrator, whom Moorman believes to progress through stages to an acceptance of death.

Nelson, Cary. "*Pearl*: the circle as figural space." In *The Incarnate Word: Literature as Verbal Space*. Urbana: University of Illinois Press, 1973, 25–49. A study of the poetic space in *Pearl,* one that is sometimes arcane and overly theoretical, but far more useful and sound as a reading of the poem than Marti's (see above) and years ahead of the current discussion of symbolic literary spatiality.

"The Pearl": A New Translation and Interpretation. Edited and translated by Sister Mary Vincent Hillman, with an introduction by Edward Vasta. Notre Dame, Ind.: University of Notre Dame Press, 1961. Although it offers a convenient and inexpensive text, with a facing-page translation, I find this edition all but useless, owing to its excessively theological and allegorical reading of the poem.

Robertson, D. W., Jr. "The Pearl as a Symbol." *Modern Language Notes* 45 (1950): 155–61. Reprinted in Conley, 18–26. Probably the more useful of the two articles Robertson contributed to this anthology. Provides scriptural and exegetical background for the poem and analyzes the poem's meaning in light of them.

Cleanness

Kelly, T. D., and John T. Irwin. "The Meaning of *Cleanness*: Parable as Effective Sign." *Mediaeval Studies* 35 (1973): 232–60. Although sometimes overly allegorical, this is still a solid analysis of *Cleanness's* "sacramental structure and parable form"—to my knowledge the first study to see some of the theoretical depth and aesthetic sophistication of this neglected poem.

Means, Michael. "The Homiletic Structure of *Cleanness*." *Studies in Medieval Culture* 5 (1975): 165–72. An extensive argument for reading *Cleanness* as a sermon in its structure and purpose, an argument that I find thoroughly unconvincing, but an important representative of a different critical approach from mine (and one of the few studies of this neglected poem).

Morse, Charlotte C. *The Pattern of Judgment in the "Queste" and "Cleanness."* Columbia: University of Missouri Press, 1978. An insightful and extensive study of *Cleanness,* and of the French prose romance *The Quest of the Holy Grail.* Morse's basic position is that divine judgment provides both the subject and also the structure of *Cleanness,* while the image of the vessel is the key to understanding humanity's role.

Patience

Andrew, Malcolm. "Jonah and Christ." *Modern Philology* 70 (1972–73): 230–33. Basically a figural reading of the poem, which I and others think invalid.

Diekstra, F. N. M. "Jonah and *Patience*: The Psychology of a Prophet." *English Studies* 55 (1974): 205–17. A very different reading of Jonah from mine, more psychological than I think merited.

Hill, Ordelle G. "The Audience of *Patience.*" *Modern Philology* 66 (1968): 103–9. Hill's thesis is that *Patience* is a poem for and about preachers; I am afraid I agree with neither the thesis nor many of the readings used to support the thesis.

Kirk, Elizabeth. "'Who Suffreth More Than God?': Narrative Redefinition of Patience in *Patience* and *Piers Plowman.*" In *The Triumph of Patience,* edited by Gerald J. Schiffhorst, 88–104. Orlando, Fla.: University Presses of Florida, 1978. A good discussion of the way the poet uses his narrative to redefine the virtue of patience.

Prior, Sandra Pierson. "*Patience*—Beyond Apocalypse." *Modern Philology* 83 (1986): 337–48. Much, though not quite all, of my argument in this article is included here in my chapter on *Patience.*

Schleusner, Jay. "History and Action in *Patience.*" *PMLA* 86 (1971): 959–65. An important essay on the role of salvation history in the poem; one that is, for me, completely convincing.

Vantuono, William. "The Structure and Sources of *Patience.*" *Mediaeval Studies* 34 (1972): 401–21. Although I disagree with most of what Vantuono says about the structure of the poem, this is a full (if to my mind wrong) analysis of the homilectic structure of this poem and much like the one by Means on *Cleanness.*

Sir Gawain and the Green Knight

Benson, Larry D. *Art and Tradition in "Sir Gawain and the Green Knight."* New Brunswick, N.J.: Rutgers Unversity Press, 1965. An earlier close study of the sources and stylistic and poetic craft of this poem. Although occasionally guilty of the New Critic's sin of overreading, this work is also characterized by New Criticism's strength: close attention to the poetic text.

Bercovitch, Sacvan. "Romance and Anti-Romance in *Sir Gawain and the Green Knight.*" *Philological Quarterly* 44 (1965): 30–37. Reprinted in Howard and Zacher, 257–66. An analysis of the "comic-realistic spirit" manifested in the poem's "anti-romance elements" (257)—a good corrective to the overly moralized readings prevalent at the time.

Borroff, Marie. "*Sir Gawain and the Green Knight*": A Stylistic and Metrical Study. New Haven, Conn.: Yale University Press, 1962. A somewhat daunting and scholarly study of the poet's style and versification, probably more useful in small doses, but nonetheless very informed and informative.

———. "*Sir Gawain and the Green Knight*: The Passing of Judgment." Reprinted in Baswell and Sharpe, 105–28. A good discussion of what I consider a very important aspect of this poem: its conflicting values and judgments.

Burrow, John A. *A Reading of "Sir Gawain and the Green Knight."* New York: Barnes and Noble, 1966. A New Criticism reading of the poem that is solid, sensible, and sensitive—for me, in no way dated, even though it is more than a quarter of a century old.

Fisher, Sheila. "Leaving Morgan Aside: Women, History, and Revisionism in *Sir Gawain and the Green Knight.*" In Baswell and Sharpe, 129–51. An engaging and provocative feminist reading of the poem.

Hanning, Robert W. "Sir Gawain and the Red Herring: The Perils of Interpretation." In Carruthers and Kirk, 5–23. An insightful discussion of the poem's "perils of interpretation" argued through outstanding close analysis of some key passages.

Harwood, Britton J. "*Gawain* and the Gift." *PMLA* 106 (1991): 483–99. A recent article that brings cultural studies to bear on the apparent "aristocratic-Christian conflict," which Harwood believes is only superficial.

Heng, Geraldine. "Feminine Knots and the Other *Sir Gawain and the Green Knight.*" *PMLA* 106 (1991): 500–54. A highly feminist reading that relies heavily on recent feminist criticism and terminology.

Hieatt, A. Kent. "*Sir Gawain*: Pentangle, *Luf-Lace,* Numerical Structure." *Papers on Language and Literature* 4 (1968): 339–59. One of the best, and certainly the most readable and most sensible, of the numerological studies of the Pearl poet.

Howard, Donald R. "Structure and Symmetry in *Sir Gawain.*" *Speculum* 39 (1964): 425–33. Reprinted in Howard and Zacher, 159–63. Intelligent and important discussion of a key aspect of the poet's art.

Howard, Donald R. and Christian K. Zacher, eds. *Critical Studies of "Sir Gawain and the Green Knight."* Notre Dame, Ind.: University of Notre Dame Press, 1968. A good representation of the critical views of 25 years ago (and more, since all are reprints); many of the essays are still useful today.

Jonassen, Frederick B. "Elements from the Traditional Drama of England in *Sir Gawain and the Green Knight.*" *Viator* 17 (1986): 221–54. A comprehensive analysis of the elements of the drama in the poem. Jonassen finds the Mummers' Play to have been especially influential, arguing that it is the source for the poem's holiday mixture of gaiety and seriousness.

Loomis, Laura Hibbard. "*Gawain and the Green Knight.*" In *Arthurian Literature in the Middle Ages: A Collaborative History,* edited by Roger Sherman Loomis, 528–40. Oxford: Oxford University Press, 1959. Reprinted in Howard and Zacher, 3–23. Useful primarily for its discussion of the poem's sources and analogues.

Mann, Jill. "Price and Value in *Sir Gawain and the Green Knight.*" *Essays in Criticism* 36 (1986): 294–318. Less valuable than Shoaf's earlier study on a similar topic, this article discusses the importance of mercantile culture and assumptions in the poem—ignoring (to its considerable disadvantage in my opinion) the poem's artistry, humor, and elements of romance.

Renoir, Alain. "Descriptive Techniques in *Sir Gawain and the Green Knight.*" *Orbis Litterarum: International Review of Literary Studies* 13 (1958): 126–32. The earlier of two fascinating articles this specialist in film wrote about the poet's visual techniques. More recent work—Hanning's article and Stanbury's book, for example—are useful supplements, but not replacements, for Renoir's early discussion of one of the most distinctive aspects of the Pearl poet's art.

————. "The Progressive Magnification: An Instance of Psychological Description in *Sir Gawain and the Green Knight.*" *Moderna Språk* 54 (1960): 245–53. The second of Renoir's two important articles (see above).

Shoaf, R. A. *The Poem as Green Girdle: Commercium in "Sir Gawain and the Green Knight."* University of Florida Monographs in the Humanities, no. 55. Gainesville: University of Florida Press, 1984. A comprehensive study of the aspects of mercantile culture in the poem, one that relies on historical context and close study of the poem itself, by a knowledgeable and interesting scholar.

————. "The 'Syngne of Surfet' and the Surfeit of Signs in *Sir Gawain and the Green Knight.*" In Baswell and Sharpe, 152–69. Drawing on Shoaf's interest in cultural background and his knowledge of sign theory, this essay gives interesting readings of some critical passages in the poem.

Silverstein, Theodore. "Sir Gawain, Dear Brutus and Britain's Fortunate Founding: A Study of Comedy and Convention." *Modern Philology* 62 (1965): 189–206. A valuable essay that focuses on the poem's historical and romantic setting.

Stevens, Martin. "Laughter and Game in *Sir Gawain and the Green Knight.*" *Speculum* 47 (1972): 65–78. An excellent reading of the poem, and a useful corrective to overly moralistic analyses.

Thiébaux, Marcelle. "Sir Gawain, the Fox Hunt, and Henry of Lancaster." *Neuphilologische Mitteilungen* 71 (1970): 469–79. Drawing on certain aspects of the fox hunt in *Gawain,* Thiébaux argues for a connection (probably as poet to patron) between the Pearl poet and Henry of Lancaster (who was John of Gaunt's father-in-law).

Index

Adam, fall of, 58
Allegory, 21, 23, 25, 80–81, 86, 137n8
Alliteration, 17, 87
Alliterative Morte Arthure, 98
Alliterative verse, 10, 14, 15–16, 17–20,
    21, 29, 33; in *Cleanness*, 59; in
    Gawain, 129; vs. syllabic verse, 17
Anglo-Saxon, 10, 14, 17; poetry, 18–20
Apocalypse, 22, 65–66, 74, 77, 81, 84,
    136n2; vs. Beatitudes, 78; and the
    New Jerusalem, 27, 28, 48
Arthur, 10, 15, 92, 93, 97, 98, 102, 107.
    See also Romances, Arthurian; Pearl
    poet: *Sir Gawain and the Green Knight*
Ashburnham House, 2
Augustine: *Christian Doctrine*, 45

Beatitudes, 78–81
Belshazzar's Feast, 62–66, 70, 71, 89
Beowulf, 2, 10
Béroul: *Tristan*, 93
Bible, translations of, 13, 16, 128
Boethius: *Consolation of Philosophy*, 23, 24,
    25, 29, 44, 50
Borroff, Marie, 16
Breton lay, 10–11
Burrow, J. A., 3, 16, 100; *Ricardian
    Poetry*, 100

Caritas, 38, 43, 44, 94, 112
Celtic language/tradition, 10–12, 14; and
    dream poem, 22; and vernacular liter-
    ature, 11–12
Chaucer, Geoffrey, 3, 4, 5, 8, 24, 128;
    The Book of the Duchess, 130; *The
    Canterbury Tales*, 6, 7, 15, 131; dialect
    used, 9; dream vision, 130; *The Legend
    of Good Women*, 23, 130, 133n2;
    Parliament of Fowls, 15; *Troilus and
    Criseyde*, 6, 130; verse forms used, 14,
    16
Chickering, Howell, 6
Chivalry, 6–8, 95, 107, 108, 110, 127.
    See also Romances, courtly

Chrétien de Troyes, 11, 96, 97, 100, 114,
    130; *Lancelot*, 115, 116; *Yvain*, 99,
    115, 143n6
Christianity, medieval, 24, 27–29, 66. *See
    also* Pearl poet: *Cleanness*, Incarnation
    passage
Christine de Pisan, 24; *Le Livre des daits
    d'armes et de chevalerie*, 6–7
Cloud of Unknowing, The, 12
Concatenation, 31–32, 36
Cosmology, medieval, 35–36
Cotton, Sir Robert, 1–2
Courtesy books, 7
Cupiditas, 37–38, 43, 94, 123
Cycle drama, 13, 14, 129, 141n14

Daniel, biblical prophet, 63, 65, 75
Dante: *Divine Comedy*, 44, 50
Dream of Scipio, 22, 24, 136n3
Dream poem, 13, 15, 21, 22–24

Edward III, 4, 6
Elegies, 10, 21, 25
Eliot, T. S., 131
English language, 8–14, 98; Celtic influ-
    ence on, 10–12; changes in, 9, 14,
    18
Eschatology, 75–77, 78
Eucharist, 69

Feminist criticism, 93, 94
Fisher, Sheila: "Leaving Morgan Aside,"
    93
Flood story, 58–60
Froissart, Jean, 24; *Chronicles*, 6, 134n9

Garter, Order of, 6, 134n8
Gawain, 1, 92, 93, 98–99, 108–27; and
    Arthur's kingdom, 99; as legend, 97;
    journey of, 112–15, 127; and the
    "luflace," 125–27; seduction of,
    116–23. *See also* Pearl poet: *Sir
    Gawain and the Green Knight*

159

The Author

Sandra Pierson Prior is with the Department of English and Comparative Literature at Columbia University, where she directs the composition program and teaches medieval literature. She has published articles on the Pearl poet and on Chaucer and has recently completed another book on the Pearl poet, entitled *The Fayre Formez of the Pearl Poet*.